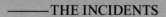

——THE INCIDENTS

DEMOCRACY AND URBAN FORM

by **RICHARD SENNETT**

————November 4, 12, 18,
and December 2, 9, 16, 1981
Piper Auditorium
Gund Hall
Harvard University
Graduate School of Design

————From the Special Collections at the Frances Loeb
Library ————Preface by Diane E. Davis ————Introduced
by Moshe Safdie ————Published by Harvard Design Press
and Sternberg Press

Editors' Note

This volume of The Incidents features six public lectures deliv-
ered by Richard Sennett at the Harvard University Graduate
School of Design in the fall of 1981. The text published here
is sourced and edited from lecture transcriptions archived at the
Special Collections at the Frances Loeb Library. This marks
the first archival volume of the series.

Contents

Diane E. Davis

These six lectures given at the Harvard University Graduate School of Design (GSD) in 1981 by the renowned sociologist Richard Sennett, on the theme of democracy and urban form, is cause for celebration. This is not just because history matters. Or because democracy matters. Or even because historical reflections on democracy and where it resides in the city have and will continue to be topics of significance and urgency for present and future generations. When Richard offered his sweeping, intellectually expansive insights into how and why design professionals need to better understand political and sociological theory if they are going to produce the cities and spaces that lead to freedom and democracy, he raised the bar for all design schools, not merely the GSD. He gave our students a chance to move beyond the technique-driven curricular training that prioritizes materials assembly, construction practices, visual and drafting skills, and design innovations. While recognizing their obvious importance, he also asked— or shall I say inspired—young design professionals to think ethically, critically, and responsibly about which kinds of cities and societies they could be producing if they understood how individuals and groups relate to the spaces that they as professionals are designing. Written almost two decades before the long-heralded phrase that the world is becoming increasingly urban, Richard used literature, philosophy, and principles of the Enlightenment, at times coupled with attention to how these ideas later engaged with theories and practices of modernization so dear to the heart of architects and designers, to open new avenues of understanding into good city form and the looming challenges that come with the growth of cities as sites of cosmopolitanism and difference.

From the vantage point of 2024, nothing seems more urgent. Cities continue to grow, but they are expanding in ways that produce exclusive high-rise towers situated in privileged neighborhoods where the financialization of land makes all but the richest unable to have access to most aesthetically pioneering architectural projects. In the last decade, we have also seen an explosion of gated communities, unequal transit access, and property trends that give those with wealth and assets advantages unavailable to the urban poor. That houselessness and inequality have reached new heights in New York City, the subject of much of Richard's reflections, as well as in Boston and across the United States should itself be a warning that we may need to go back to the basics and focus on people and the social relations they create in order to revive urban livability. Granted, everything Richard discussed in these original lectures is not as relevant today as it was in 1981. Richard was recounting the city as understood from his personal vantage point, using that as a basis for reflecting on urban social and political theory, with both passion and urgency. Some of his original observations or projections may even appear dated, because that is the nature of cities and their residents: they are always changing and transforming. But when Richard revealed how and why urban form has a bearing on individuals' capacities to produce or experience inclusive communities of allegiance built on spatial engagement, urban serendipity, and the ephemeral attachments that tie strangers to each other, he not only asked our students to think about the social consequences of the myriad design decisions made by architects, urban designers, and planners. He also gave hope that if one kept these and other sociological principles in mind, they could be used to strengthen democracy, albeit through design visioning and spatial imagination.

As we move into a bitterly divided time in our society, where political allegiances are built on the othering of those with different races, nationalities, social class, and even education—and where someone can be killed for entering a neighborhood where they are assumed to not belong—we must keep these ideas in our hearts, minds, and hands. Urban futures can be made better, and that is precisely why the principles and lessons embodied in these lectures are timeless.

DEMOCRACY DISABLED

MOSHE SAFDIE: It is a pleasure to present Richard Sennett. Richard was born in 1943 in Chicago. He spent considerable time in France during his youth, then came back to Chicago where he graduated in music history, and then went to the Juilliard School, where he has a degree in conducting. He has his PhD from Harvard in American Studies, which, as he puts it, was the only way one could really get into urban history. He is presently professor of sociology at New York University and director of the New York Institute of Humanities. He's also taught at Harvard, Brandeis, King's College, and the College de France. His major books are *The Uses of Disorder*, *The Fall of Public Man*, *Authority*, *Families Against the City*, and *Hidden Injuries of Class*, which is about Boston. His novel, *The Frog Who Dared to Croak*, is forthcoming. ——— Richard Sennett is a very keen observer of cities, and I had an opportunity recently to see that. He accompanied a group of Harvard GSD students for two weeks in Jerusalem as part of our Jerusalem Studies program, and upon his return he sent me his journal, which is to be published at the *New Yorker*. I was amazed to see that after two weeks, never having been there, he knew and understood more about the city than many natives. ———— This is the first of six lectures, which are together entitled "Democracy and Urban Form." I believe it a significant and timely event for the Harvard GSD, and I think it is appropriate to open the series by explaining why the subject of these lectures is of particular significance at this moment in this School. These are bewildering times for urbanism and architecture. It is a period of search and reexamination. We have come to realize that the modern movement, in its urge to cleanse and purify the city, metaphorically and practically, abandoned traditional urban structures— the streets, the public place, the piazza, the square, the market, the urban garden—for alternative urban forms that at first appeared to be utopian, and soon proved to deny the substance upon which urban life depends. In a panic of this realization, we returned to the study and embrace exploration of urban structures and patterns of the past. It somehow seems that in the urge to fill the vacuum, we have quite indiscriminately begun adopting

THE INCIDENTS

models without the understanding that each model was a response to a particular society in a particular period of its evolution: it is an echo of the distribution of power, of authority, of lifestyle, of available resources, of prevalent technologies, and of distribution of income, to mention only a few of the social-economic and political forces that shaped the city. ——— The proof of this apparent direction can be demonstrated in design studios, be it be our studios here at the GSD or at any school across the country. For the first time in many decades, we can walk around the studio and see students working on their designs while sitting with open books, relating to historical references as a guide. It is quite fascinating to see that for a single particular design problem, you can see some students looking at Hadrian's Villa, others looking at seventeenth-century Italian cities, others have a little piece of an eighteenth-century French city, and others yet with models from nineteenth-century Austria, with an appropriate sprinkling of Isfahan and further east. ——— That we cast our nets so widely for such models into a study of contemporary urbanism suggests the extent we have come to dissociate them from the societies that generated them, and the pessimism we have of the relevance of our times to generate urban forms today. Nowhere is that clearer than in our attitude toward symbolic issues. In the cleansing or purifying phase of the modern movements—*puritanical* might be a better word—many rich and meaningful facets of the environment are suppressed. Having come to realize this we similarly cast a wide net, convinced that wherever we fish can fill the vacuum that we feel. But symbols like urban forms grow from within society. They are often universal; at least, they are expressions of collective agreement—not a private personal matter. ———— Richard Sennett has devoted a lifetime to exploring these connections between form and life. I am sure that these six lectures are destined to become significant events. Please welcome Richard Sennett.

RICHARD SENNETT: The subject of these lectures is how the form of cities and the way cities are used encourages or discourages democratic processes. I shall explore this subject by connecting the visual and the political. This relation between the visual and the political has a curious general history. Up until quite recently, people who designed cities and individual buildings thought about the social consequences of what they were doing, and quite explicitly so, for instance in the work of Leon Battista Alberti. From the other side, people who thought about political philosophy often also thought about how their ideas would look literally, as in the case of Jean-Jacques Rousseau's *The Social Contract*. In the last two or three generations, this connection between the visual and the political grew weaker. On the side of social philosophy, the eye and its vision cease to be important. And on the side of urban planning, the social consequences of architecture and urban design have become mostly a matter of thinking in cliches— cliches of human scale, community, and participation, without much consideration of what these words mean. These lectures aim to recover a certain tradition and to reestablish a connection. I'm going to disappoint you if you think I shall or could give a comprehensive theory, or a neat and symmetrical connection between the political and the visual. The further I get into the subject the more difficult and confusing it becomes to me.

The foundation of any democratic order is discourse. Not canned information or pretty political advertisements, but talk, back and forth. The assumption is that talk will change what people think, that they will discover something by discourse, and that they will be confronted with beings who are different. A good theory of democracy must be based on what might be pompously called the *transformational power of discourse*. More simply stated, it might just be said that talking leads people to an appreciation of difference. Even if someone retains his or her original belief, the belief should be encountered, and should be enriched by the encounter with difference. The belief acquires its meaning by placing it in a context unlike the context one imagines for oneself. The problems that come out of this fundamental importance are: Who is entitled to talk? What is allowed or forbidden to be discussed? Most importantly, what is discussable? That is, what is capable of being put into words?

The city has an intimate twofold relation to this democratic foundation. First of all, cities have historically been the places that bring large numbers of people together in a dense space. Cities concentrate people. Lots of them. A special environment for talking is created, if people do it, which is different in kind than talking in a family, or talking with neighbors, all of whom one's family has known for generations in the same village. Secondly, cities bring, or have brought historically, different kinds of people together. Cities create a special environment for democratic exchanges because of their size, by virtue of the richness of the different kinds of people who live in them; this environment furnishes the subject for democratic speech: differences and similarities. If you believe in the democratic principle and the transformative power during discourse, then the city is a unique environment in which to practice this principle. That is, with more richness and more difference to be explored than in a small town, it represents therefore a higher stage of democracy than the talk of, say, a New England town meeting. If, that is, the discourse about difference occurs.

Several writers writing about cities have perceived that this democratic ideal is something very disturbing, even tragic. Aristotle for instance believed that eventually talk in the city would be unified, and its differences ironed out. And then the city would be on a course to death: democracy would be the means to unity, unity would destroy the sense of needing to say anything further to one another, and a single ruler, an autarch or autarchus, would take over. Small-scale democracy is self-destructive. Vigorous democratic discourse is unsettling in that it is not a principle of political order; such for instance was the idea of Benjamin Constant, which he deduced from his experiences in Paris during the Great Revolution. ———
I don't know if a modern democratic society will suffer the fate of ancient Athens, but I do know vigorous democracy is feared because it is unsettling or destabilizing. This fear has become a potent tool in the modern world for preventing people from freedom of expression. And I believe that it is better to attempt to create this freedom of discourse and then deal with its consequences than to shun democratic freedom in advance because it might be anarchic.

Modern cities are designed and used in such a way as to strangle the possibilities for democracy. First, both in their design and the way people want to use cities, places for encounter and discourse are being destroyed. A reign of isolation, silence, and static information is being substituted. Secondly, the means by which cities generate human differences, concentrate these differences, and expose them is being replaced by the theory and practice of cultural segregation. I could not and would not claim that we are destroying a democratic Valhalla that has existed before in the wonderful past. In fact, my position is just absolutely the opposite: that indeed, never before has the possibility for democracy been potentially stronger thanks to the breakdown of organic village life and rigid family roles. These were tremendously powerful inward-turning forces, and we're free of them, but we don't know what to do with the potential freedom. Far from regretting the kind of dissolution of an organic community, it's something that gives us wonderful and unique freedom, but we don't know how to use it.

If I might put this another way, which I want to say particularly to the architects here, never have the potential political consequences of architecture been greater, and never has the political sensibility of architecture been less. ——— As this is in the way of general introduction, I've had to present my theme in very abstract terms. Let me just briefly share the plan of these lectures and then come to the body of my talk today. The first four lectures are diagnoses of how discourse and difference are constricted and reduced in modern cities. The last two are some ideas about what might be done to unconstrict and increase discourse.

Today we are going to explore how the imposition of silence became the tool of order in the modern city. Next week, we are going to consider the meaning of the theory of democracy. Alexis de Tocqueville offers a very powerful theory, which argues that in a modern democracy people desire isolation— it isn't just imposed on them, but people want to be alone, and they fear discourse from those who are most unlike themselves. In the third lecture, we will explore the aesthetics of isolation. How can even simple architectural details desensitize people to the presence of social differences? I want to consider this problem in relation to the theory of urban desensitization put forward in the beginning of the twentieth century by the sociologist Georg Simmel. In the fourth lecture I want to explore what seems to be a false remedy for urban isolation and silence, that is, the remedy of small-scale community. I want to talk particularly about the politics of identity in cities. The fifth lecture will explore different kinds of urban form in communities. The last lecture will try to assay which of these forms enable democratic discourse in cities.

We'll thus move from four discussions that are concrete and critical to two discussions that will be I hope equally concrete, even though more utopian. By the way, what I'd like to do since there are so many people is—I don't think it will work to have a discussion of this lecture immediately after it. But I will be here tomorrow morning say around nine, and if any of you are free and you'd like to discuss this, please come to Room 510, and bring cups of coffee since that's an ungodly hour, and we can have discourse about this period of discourse. ———
So let me begin today with an analysis of the planning of silence in modern cities. In the middle of the nineteenth century, planners began an attempt to build silence into the very fabric of the city. They sought to do so principally by isolating physically social groups that might come into conflict, like workers from the bourgeois, or different ethnic groups, assuming that a lack of contact decreases conflict. They sought to ensure political order in the city by this isolation, to remove street confrontations that might flare up and sustain revolutionary upheavals. Those who were different would not be allowed to speak to one another.

The great example in the last century of planning political stability through creating silence appeared in the rebuilding of Paris in the 1850s and 1860s. The rebuilding occurred under the direction of Baron Georges-Eugène Haussmann, who was supported in turn by the newly enthroned Emperor, Napoleon III. It is his work that forms the legacy of nineteenth-century planning for our own time. ——— After the Revolution of 1848, few people doubted that Paris was in need of some sort of renewal. Many streets had been physically destroyed during the revolutionary events. Paris was the city of the *ancien régime*, and its transport systems, sanitary engineering, and housing stock were beginning to feel the population and economic pressures of modern life. To walk from the corner of Boulevard St. Germain and the Boulevard Raspail to the Place des Vosges, which today takes about 40 minutes, took two hours in 1850 because of the twisted and often unconnected street pattern in the city.

The question was not whether to renew the city, but how to do it. When Haussmann began his work in 1853, he later recalled, "The Emperor," that's Napoleon III, "was anxious to show me a map of Paris, on which one saw traced by Himself," *himself* capitalized, "in blue, red, yellow, and green, according to their degree of urgency, the different new routes he proposed to have undertaken." This is what power meant to both Haussmann and Napoleon III—the power of mapping: the power to enforce a mapped image of the city upon the living organism of the city. Mapping has ruled city-making since ancient times, but it became more destructive. The line is drawn on paper by someone, the street is then demolished or altered to fit the line. Napoleon III gave Haussmann the power to move from the pen to the wrecking ball. The people in the streets and communities were given little opportunity to help draw the maps.

Evenement du 12 Juillet 1789 à six heures du Soir.

Le Prince Lambese entrant dans les Thuilleries le Sabre à la main, avec un Detachement de son Regiment, Royal Almand, abbat à ses Pieds un Veillard et fait fuir tous les Citoyens qui se promenent.

Foreign troops in the service of the King charge the Parisian populace at the Tuileries, 1789.

Haussmann Plans of Paris, 1853–70.

THE INCIDENTS

More broadly, Haussmann made the concrete exercise of this autocratic power a matter of subjecting the city to geometry. Haussmann wrote of his subordinates that they erected "a great wooden mast, higher than the highest houses, and perched like pigeons on these masts," they "measured according to the methods of triangulation, by means of the most perfect precision instruments, the angles formed by each of the sides of the triangle determined on the spot by the extension of the central shafts of these temporary structures." That's important language. Geometry as he used it did not account for the irregular mess of growth over the course of history, and thus legitimated the destruction of neighborhoods. A more benign geometry in cities had long before animated French architects and planners. In the Renaissance, it goes back to the ideas like the star-shaped city, where the formal geometries establish perimeters but left the space free within. Later, Claude-Nicolas Ledoux, whose designs foreshadow the writings on rationalized labor of St. Simon, also did not try to rationalize the spaces of the city.

Haussmann thought more geometrically because he was driven more politically. Politics appeared to him in the first instance matters of removing opposition to progress, an argument we're very familiar with, and in the second instance of giving the city form. From this complete geometry, each social piece of the design could be filled in logically. This autocratic geometry is out of fashion today. Most liberal planners believe that people who inhabit an environment should participate in its design. But the uses to which Haussmann put his powers remain an enduring if disguised force of the planning of cities. It is the use rather than the form of his power that constitutes his legacy to our time. The geometer of Paris joined the political order and silenced planning the city in four ways. ———— The first is the relationship of the Grande Boulevard to the sections behind it. The second is the building of the socioeconomically homo-geneous house. The third is the development of homogeneous neighborhoods—the new tool of real estate investing. The fourth is the street, in which free motion because an absolute, and space becomes dependent on motion.

The city of Palmanova.

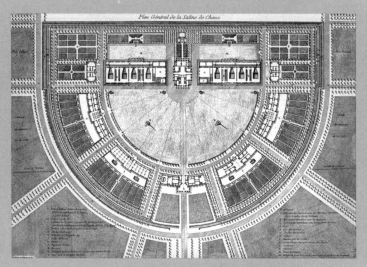

Claude-Nicolas Ledoux, the Ideal City of Chaux,
general plan, 1774–78.

Haussmann's first effort was to create new wide streets, which cut through some of the oldest and poorest quarters of the city. Such streets as the Rue de Rennes on the left bank or the Avenue de l'Opera on the right bank gutted working-class quarters. It's hard for us to imagine today because they are now so chic, but these were working-class centers 140 years ago. The public justification for these streets was that the new street would become a lung for the congested quartier, providing light and fresh air into the poor. To his colleagues Haussmann spoke of other advantages. Troops and artillery could quickly be moved down along the straight streets. They were a good way to combat the building of barricades in the working-class quartier. Barricades are the principal strategic device European working classes had used to cope with the superior military might of the government during all three previous revolutionary upheavals. Haussmann spoke of the advantage of one such street as "a spacious, direct, monumental, and above all, a strategic route." The city fathers spoke in similar terms about the extension of the Rue de Rivoli two years before Haussmann had assumed almost dictatorial control.

He had the sort of control that Robert Moses longed for and dreamed of. Here's what the city fathers said: "The interests of public order, not less those of salubrity, demand that a wide swath be cut as soon as possible across this district of barricades, an intermediate line will be added to the great strategic line of the boulevard." In the words of Anthony Vidler, a modern analyst of Haussmann's regime, order within Paris became the first practically symbolic step in establishing order within the French empire as a whole. Haussmann himself became increasingly bold in announcing his theme. He spoke of the "disemboweling of the old Paris, of the quarter of riots in Paris." Now, the street as a military route had a direct social consequence. It cut off places of assembly for the working classes in the city. If a crowd assembled to listen to a street orator, police or troops could quickly be rushed to the trouble spots, so that the crowd could be dispersed. Discipline and silence among the masses was thus enforced by urban geometry.

This way of building streets had an economic consequence. Not only did it isolate the poor from each other and make it possible to silence them quickly if they met spontaneously, but it also isolated the poor from the middle classes. The shops and apartments of the Grandes Boulevard were meant for the middle classes. They were lines of respectability laid down for the working class of Paris. A lady in her carriage on the Avenue de l'Opera saw no squalid scenes of poverty as she traveled along the streets; she only saw enticing shops and decorous apartment dwellers. The poor were hidden from sight. Human beings, that is, were less and less able to learn with their eyes about social differences on these streets. Social contacts between the classes decreased. Thus did Haussmann's concept of the street isolate the poor from each other and from the middle class.

The second major step he took in creating order through isolation appeared in the building of new houses in Paris. The housing stock of ancient regime Paris had, by the middle of the nineteenth century, become mixed, often widely so. Old private mansions after the great revolution had often been cut up so that very rich families would occupy a suite of rooms next to very poor families. For instance, the piano nobile would be inhabited by the rich and the antechambers would be walled and inhabited by the poor. A great change in housing in Paris in the first half of the nineteenth century was the carving up of these private dwellings into apartments. Whether the private dwellings were mansions or more modest homes, they were carved up in this haphazard way. After 1830 this confusion increased in certain quartiers, like in the north end of the fifth arrondissment just to the east of the Place Saint-Michel.

Now, Haussmann sought to bring order to Parisian real estate by planning houses more coherently, that is, to make each floor in new housing for a particular class. The rich on the first floor, the less wealthy on the floor next, up to the servants in the attic. This vertical segregation was a tendency in housing construction from the middle of the eighteenth century onward. He didn't invent it, but Haussmann sought to convert this tendency into a rigid rule. Moreover, he sought to squeeze the working classes out of the spectrum of those installed in the new houses, so that the houses registered shades of the middle class by floors, with the attics reserved for the servants of all those who resided immediately below. Most importantly, Haussmann sought to reduce the intermingling of functions of the traditional Parisian apartment house by moving craftsmen and light industry to the courtyards, and restrict the shops and street fronts to "genteel trades." He wrote, "Silence and peace is to be prized at home. A prime gain by separating family life from labor." In other words, the separation of work and home as it becomes institutionalized in the nineteenth century is for the sake of order—that is, in order created through silence. There won't be any noisy shops downstairs and there won't be any servants coming and going. Everything in the house belongs in the house as a refuge.

Now, this effort to build a more socially homogeneous house was extended to the building of whole new neighborhoods. This was Haussmann's third building strategy, which grew out of his second. When Haussmann set out to build a new quartier around the Parc Monceau or near Noilly or near Les Batignolles or along the Avenue de Wagram—do you know that the Place de l'Etoile, which, since 1970, was known as Place Charles de Gaulle, and Avenue du Wagram, which goes north of it, is all entirely new and entirely built by him—he sought to build neighborhoods in which everyone came of the same class. The housing stock pitched to the tastes and pockets of a particular band of the middle classes indeed.

The economic reason for this was that mass housing at a single scale meant builders could order massive amounts of the same quantities and materials. Uniformity meant volume purchase, and thus lowered their costs. The social reason for these neighborhoods was that they made the residents feel secure. The sense of security was more than a matter of being removed from the poor: by living only with people at the same level as yourself, you weren't subject to "humiliations from your betters" nor exposed to the vulgarities of those below you in the social scale, whom you would be disposed to snub in turn. You were "chez soi," isolated from others, but known to yourself by being among equals.

The last form of order through social isolation Haussmann created was in the speed people moved through Parisian streets. Haussmann and his colleagues tried to make free motion an absolute value in these streets. The faster you could move down a street, the better planned the street was. In other words, the street as a space to dwell in became subordinate to motion.

——— In terms of the history of city planning, this premium put on motion was Haussmann's most radical departure. Haussmann, in the words of Françoise Choay, conceived a network of through streets that have no signification in themselves but are essentially a means of connections. Haussmann himself recognized that he was involved in a massive effort to annihilate space as it was formerly experienced in cities. He spoke of the large new plazas built by the intersections of these new streets as "nodes of relation." There were not places to be in but pass through.

It was a well-known characteristic of Haussmann's that he hated cafes and would have closed as many as possible if he could. He was a visionary of the fast-food shop and of the drive-in. Motion became the ultimate tool of isolation. The premium put on motion devalued the space human beings inhabit together as a meeting ground and as in itself worthwhile. Instead, there are only nodes of connection to the traffic. ——— From the Greeks on, the planning of cities was oriented to giving city residents a sense that they inhabited a special milieu in which they could come into contact with each other—admire each other or make nasty observations—and in which the buildings were spaces with a life of their own. A contemporary critic of Haussmann's work, Victor Fornelle, described in 1865 the change in the sense of habitation Haussmann caused. Paris under Haussmann lost "the picturesqueness, the variety, the unexpectedness, the charm of discovery, which made a walk in old Paris an exploratory voyage through always new and always unknown worlds, a multiple and living physiognomy that gave each district of the city its special traits, like those of a human face." Less romantic critics like Adolphe Thiers and Émile Zola observed simply that the sense of having a life in common with other people was diminished.

These four expressions of the great geometer's planning—great streets that cut through and divided old sections of the city by making streets, homogeneous houses, homogeneous neighborhoods, and space subordinate to motion—reveal ideas about control and power in the city that endure today: first, that the tensions between social classes are best handled by separating them, that is, that the more social contact, the more likely a political explosion; second, the ideological formulation of power was the union of economical rationality to homogeneity; and third, the devaluation of public life through making space subordinate to motion.

All four of Haussmann's planning devices attempt to defuse class conflict through reducing class contact. Which, translated politically, means the police can be quickly moved down the boulevard when crowds form on the side streets. The boulevards themselves have the effect of isolating the residents living on one side of them from residents living on the other, much as modern highways cut through ghettos and have the physical effect of isolating people on either side. Down the center fast-moving traffic cuts off easy contact at the sides. A homogeneous house removes those from the premises who were not roughly of the middle class with the exception of household servants. The removal of artisan activities from the courtyard also gave the bourgeois residents the sense of living in a haven. The homogeneous neighborhoods extended the notion of insulation from jarring social differences planned in the Haussmannian apartment buildings, and the devaluation of squares as meeting grounds—the subordination of these urban spaces to the demands of rapid traffic motion—cut down the social contact people had with one another. This is a beautiful quote from Haussmann—horrifying but beautiful. "The city, uncontrolled, is like a fuse of a bomb," he once wrote. "And the compartmentalizing of the city is like dipping that fuse in water."

From the bourgeois standpoint, they lived through extraordinary revolutionary upheaval and a tremendous sense of tension every day. The technique they found was the technique of isolation, not of domination; that is to say, not wiping out the workers or driving them out of the city, but of isolation in the very construction of the city. Haussmann's planning techniques also joined in the minds of investors and city planners the idea that economic rationality depends on social homogeneity. It became common sense to believe that it was more rational to invest in a homogeneous neighborhood than a mixed neighborhood because you knew what you were getting, so-called common sense. There were no surprises, and no sudden shifts of property values, because everybody was pretty much the same. Moreover, housing could be built on a massive scale, and builders can take advantage of these volume purchases of materials. The political undertow of homogeneous planning like his is built instead on the fear that diversity in a city makes the bourgeoisie vulnerable. Ever since the first revolution, those who held power in France feared that public contact might threaten political order. The solutions before Haussmann, as in the 1810s and the late 1930s, had consisted in attempts to suppress crowd activities at the moment they seemed to turn threatening. Haussmann's solution was more radical: to prevent the formation of crowds in the first place. That is the great change in crowd control in the history of urbanism in the nineteenth century.

Nothing could be further from this than the more confident ideas of Renaissance city builders like Sixtus the Fifth, who saw in the intermingling of rich and poor homes in Rome an opportunity for the rich and powerful to dominate discipline and subdue their poorer neighbors. —————— Haussmann was not of course the only person to think in these terms. From London to Vienna, nineteenth-century developers acted on the politics and economics of homogeneity and separation of differences. But Haussmann was the first to envision a whole city built entirely this way. He was unusual in the nineteenth century because of the amount of power he possessed. The single planner under the patronage of a single man, he wielded political, economic, and technical control of a city all at once. He may have been a single villain, but represents a certain idea about the city, which took form more widely. For instance, in the building of the Ringstrasse in Vienna during the middle of the nineteenth century, a similar concern to isolate the new quarters from the old inner core of Vienna and the working districts outside the ring appeared.

Though no single theorist of order of isolation appears as a master planner. Carl E. Schorske writes of the making of the Ringstrasse: "Instead of a strong radial system, which one would expect to link the outer parts and the city center, most of the streets that enter the ring area from either inner city or suburb have little or no prominence. They debouche in the circular flow without crossing it. The old city was thus enclosed by the ring—reduced to something museum like." The effect of this isolation in the building of the Ringstrasse, Schorske says, is such that "what had been a military insulation belt became a sociological insulation belt." Now Haussmann in language appears directly and paradoxically in critics of the urban order as well as its creators. Otto Wagner, a critic of the ideal of prettifying the surface appearances of cities, an idea that governed the planning both of the Ringstrasse and Haussmann's apartment facades, could speak of the need to replace the street as a "corso, as a space to be in," by the street as an "artery, a place of circulation." It is a concept that echoes Haussmann's belief in the dominance of motion over association in the street.

A romantic like Ebenezer Howard in England could conceive of abolishing private property and instituting socialism only through withdrawing people into small units, new small towns surrounded by swaths of country, as though the very pressure of density and diversity in a cosmopolitan city would overwhelm them. Self-possession through social withdrawal, withdrawal from contact with the alien, the enemy, the formula appears in the political left in the nineteenth century and early twentieth-century town planning, as well as on the right among the guardians of the empire. Howard, for instance, imagined a very different political order than that of Haussmann, but shared with him the assumption that people who experience the complexities of social diversity of difference will be incapable of creating that order. He said that you cannot have democracy when you have confusion. On the contrary: you can only have democracy when your planning work admits confrontation, mixture, and porosity—all of which create confusion.

The word *community* seldom appears in Haussmann's writings, but it does appear in more generous spirits like Howard, who are as fearful of complexity and difference. For these more generous planners the assumption was that when you live with your own kind, you will become more politically engaged. But the engagements of communities like Howard's, where people know and understand their neighbors, are inherently undemocratic.

This is obvious and non-obvious. The first obvious legacy of Haussmann's is the suburb. The important thing to say about that legacy of the suburb is not just that the class is homogeneous but use is homogeneous. And it accomplishes the same isolating end—that is, the business strip or the shopping center separated from the residential zone, separated from the school campuses for kids, separated from the hospital campus. I mean the kind of *campusitization* of life, in which the notion is that one has created order by clearly disarticulating all these units. The non-obvious consequence of disaggregating a city into local communities is that isolation seeps into the lives of those who are alike. They do not hold together as a community but reproduce among themselves their isolation from the alien. This paradox, which is the whole theme of Tocqueville's second volume of *Democracy in America*, says that to withdraw from others who are unlike is a first step in withdrawing from others who are like.

And here is where the great historical irony of the legacy identified with Haussmann's name lies. Isolation from difference has been a consequent principle: the assumptions we now make but that we seldom think about in city planning, and indeed in the design of individual space, are imprints of this fusion of political order with silence. ———— There's the highway, and its converse, the even more hideous pedestrian mall for shopping—where you are loitering or causing a public nuisance if you give a speech, or play music as a street musician—in which you are there to shop and to be stimulated to shop. That again is a way of disaggregating forms of motion, in the case of the highway, or of making the space itself absolutely homogeneous. There's very little overlap of functions. That's why Faneuil Hall is so marvelous, because it really seems to be a very complex space. The third sort of obvious way in which planners have imbued these Haussmannian ideals are with things like the industrial park and the campuses. I should say that Haussmann was a great admirer of Cornell University. Why this particular university had such a hold over him, I don't know. But that is the notion that the industrial park is a way of creating something that is economically rational, because it's socially homogeneous, again by use.

These are obvious, and here I come to the end of this long-winded presentation. The power involved in social isolation, rationality, and public domain as instrumental means has a less obvious realization in modern urban form. I want to talk about two of them. We know that the very concept of professional planning is often a device for bureaucratic protection, isolating the urban user from exercising power over his or her life. But even if there's participation, the object built can still and often does reflect the dominant ideas of power in its Haussmannian aspects. It does so by becoming fixed, indeed a thing, an object whose form follows function.

If what you're doing is creating something that is a fixed urban object, a building that can only exist for one purpose, then you are engaged in that Haussmannian world of articulation for the sake of separation. Few urban structures are designed capable of evolving in tandem with the history of the place where they are. I mean, think of any office building. Those of you who do any practical work with planning know how difficult it is to redesign, for instance, an office building so that it becomes a high-rise apartment building. Even if the original office building was arrived at by a point of democratic participation, the object is still fixed. Of course, this seems to us economically rational, because we can identify what its program is. It's also exclusionary, since once the need for that function disappears the need for it is abandoned, be it the form of building, the neighborhood, whatever. And the result of this is what I call the migratory city, which is what I have great fears we are in danger of creating: a city in which the city migrates around space, but in which the space has ever more and more difficulty in being renewed, because it has been made into a known object. And the second import, the second way of these, of this Haussmannian intervention in the city, is the concept of the idea of discourse with the other. It's cut loose from concrete circumstances in time and place.

Again, I asserted at the outset of this talk that most democratic theory is founded on the notion of discourse. But where can you have it in a modern city? In some working-class neighborhoods you can still have it, but you can't have discourse in shopping malls. In New York we're arrested for political discussions in Queens Plaza. What happened is that this re-articulation of space has meant that discourse has been removed from the domain of spontaneous talk. When Aristotle imagined the place for discourse in the city, he imagined that this transforming power of discourse could occur, that there was freedom precisely because of the opportunity to speak spontaneously—not to be controlled by an autarch, not to have the conditions of discourse determined in advance, and when this top-down control was absent, spontaneous talk became possible. What we have is a rather different situation. We have flows of information that can be terminated the moment they're painful; that is, that pain and the possibility of pain has become the regulator of discourse. And that is as true if you turn off your radio or TV set when you hear something somebody is saying that you don't like. It is as for us as it was for those Haussmannians, who didn't want to hear workers, didn't want to see workers, and didn't want to have that possibility of spontaneous confrontation.

And finally, and most importantly, this premium on motion over space in public also blocks discourse. That is, that space is not a place to be in but to move through. In a book of mine called *The Fall of Public Man*, I tried to embody the way in which this pattern of political domination through silence is reified, or internally re-objectified, but we'll leave all that aside for later. Through the notion that has grown so strong in modern cities—when we've internalized this Haussmannian ideal— is the notion that one has the right to silence in public, that one has a right not to be accosted, that one can only defend one-self by regulating the verbal, that the right to silence becomes the pre-condition of urban protection. A notion of the right to silence, which is founded on this idea, is that contact with difference is likely to make one seem vulnerable to being hurt. And the last thing I want to say is that you'll notice in talking about this legacy that I've switched the terms from talking about a very concrete situation of the relationship between the bourgeois and working class to talking about something within the bourgeois. And I meant to do that. That is to say that this internalization, so that one tries to keep out painful otherness by these techniques of silence, of homogenization and of sep-aration, has now become the way in which we essentially have the techniques of self-dealing in cities.

We will begin the next lecture with the theorist Tocqueville, who tried to understand what that desire to withdraw from other people was about. I hope to discuss Tocqueville not as an urban theorist, since he wrote rather little about cities, but as somebody who in making this analysis about the desire to withdraw from other people has a great deal to say about the conditions of bourgeois city life today.

THE DESIRE FOR ISOLATION OUT OF FEAR

RICHARD: I have to apologize for this lecture. I had written something out, and after the seminar that we had last Friday I ripped it up. So, this lecture is rather more disorganized than I would like. I want to talk about something that is mostly in the domain of social theory; we'll get to something that is overtly visual and urban at the very end of the lecture.

——————The story up to this point is essentially a story of how isolation was imposed in the city. In terms of democracy, that imposition of isolation cuts off discourse and confrontation with others. But the imagery that we used was of the power structure forcing people apart. And this is simply too easy a politics; it presents the denizens of the city as passive victims done in by the power structure. That's not wrong, but such a notion of passivity is incomplete; people are not just passive receivers. This terrible error was not made by Marx, but a lot of very vulgar Marxists in his wake did so. But there's no interaction between those who are dominated and those who do the dominating.

What I want to look at today is that complicity. I want to look at the way in which people resist discourse with the other, and ways in which they desire isolation. It will take us far from what you may think of as architectural or urban design problems, but I hope to bring it back at the end. There is an interaction between domination and people afraid of confronting or experiencing the life of others who are unlike themselves. ———— The morality of withdrawal is one of the strongest features of New England culture, particularly in the nineteenth century. The desire to be isolated from other people, for instance, appears in a passage from Ralph Waldo Emerson's *Politics*, written in 1840.

> The appearance of character makes the
> state unnecessary. The wise man is the state,
> he needs no army, fort, or navy. He loves
> men too well. No bribe or feast or palace to
> draw friends to him, no vantage ground,
> no favorable circumstances. He needs no
> library, for he has done no thinking. No church
> for he is a prophet, no statute book for he has
> become the lawgiver, no money for he is value,
> no road for he is at home wherever he is,
> no experience for the life of the Creator shoots
> through him. He has no personal friends.

New England Transcendentalism is not the kind of voluntary withdrawal we're going to be talking about. Emerson evinced a pride of self. There's no fear in that statement of Emerson's, complex as it is in many ways. It's what Quentin Anderson wrote about in a marvelous book called *The Example of the Imperial Self*. What I what to explore is something much darker and much more painful. It's the desire to withdraw from society, because people are afraid of what will happen to them if they come into contact with people who are unlike themselves. And the questions that I want us to explore—and as I say it's going to be a mess, but just bear with me—is where this fear of others comes from. Where does the fear of coming into contact with people who are unlike you come from, and what are its consequences?

This is a vast social problem, with a twofold aspect. First, as an urban problem—resistance to busing, not wanting to live with Black people in the same neighborhood, being afraid to live with people who are poorer than you, being afraid of people who are a different ethnicity, and so on. The fear of otherness can produce those kinds of concrete problems. But to understand that urban problem I think we first of all have to understand it as a problem in democratic theory. That is, how can we have anything that is called a democracy if people don't have a desire for discourse with those who are different from themselves? The proposition I want to look at today comes from a man who said, "It is precisely democracy properly understood that causes the fear of otherness." We've been using the sense of democracy in the opening of these lectures as discourse with the other. Alexis de Toqueville asserted that democracy causes these fears in people, and results in a solitary everyday life. The structure of city life is intimately related to the democratic solitude, which is Tocqueville's great theme. But how?

I thought I'd start by trying to give you an intuitive sense of what this connection feels like. In the last lecture, we considered the dormitory suburb as an example of the social isolation imposed by planners in the Baron Haussmann tradition. The modern French equivalent of the dormitory suburb is called *un grande ensemble*. I'd like to read you two passages from a marvelous novel about these *grandes ensembles* in Paris today; written by a woman named Christiane Rochefort, called *Les Petites Enfants du Siècle*. It was published in 1961 in France, then in English the next year under the title the *Children of Heaven*. It's out of print and your library doesn't have a copy, but even so it's a superb novel. She writes about these *grandes ensembles*, that:

> At night the windows would light up and inside there were only happy families, happy families, happy families. Going by you could see them beneath the ceiling bulbs through the big picture windows, one happiness after another, all along alike as twins or a nightmare. The happinesses facing west could look out of their houses and see the happinesses that faced east, as if they were seeing themselves in a mirror. Eating noodles from the co-op, happinesses heaped one on top of the other, I could have figured out the volume in cubic feet, or in yards, or in barrels of this happiness. The wind blew over the Avron plateau—

You have to imagine a huge block of Corbusier-type buildings, with a kind of concrete plateau in the center, and they're named *plateau*, and this one is called Avron plateau.

> The wind blew over the Avron plateau. It blew
> between the apartments as in the Colorado
> Canyon, which could never be such a wilder-
> ness. Instead of coyotes at nightfall, speakers
> howled the word on how everyone could have
> white teeth and shining hair. How everyone
> could be beautiful, clean, healthy, and happy.

Power enters her story as a surveillance architecture, as in a place called Sarcelles, which is the largest and cleanest of these *grandes ensembles*. Have any of you ever seen this? Sarcelles is a Corbusier dream and a nightmare; she says about it,

> A person could do no evil here. Any kid who
> played hooky they would spot and write off.
> The only one his age, outside at the wrong time.
> A robber would show for miles away with the
> loot. Anybody dirty, people would send him off
> to wash. We were totally naked to each other,
> totally alone.

Children playing on a slide, Grand ensemble de Sarcelles
(Architects: M. Borleau and Jacques Henri-Labourdette), 1961.

Kips Bay Plaza (Architects: I. M. Pei, James Ingo Freed), 1963.

THE INCIDENTS

These passages introduce us to a theme running throughout the novel: the relationship between solitude and equality. For instance, in the passage I quoted above, the proprieties of people facing west could look out of their houses and see the propriety of people whose houses faced east as if they were seeing themselves in a mirror. We know what she is describing visually—in this country it's buildings like I. M. Pei's Turtle Bay Apartments. This endless vista of equality produces in those who inhabit them a profound feeling of solitude, as when she says, "the wind blew over the Avron plateau, it blew between the apartment buildings as in the Colorado Canyon, which could never be such a wilderness." The complexity of her novel, which rescues such descriptions from being the sort of beautiful expression of a cliche, explores the desires of Parisians coming from dense, diverse, vibrant working-class communities to live in this canyon of solitude, to where she says they "abandon themselves to health." What's interesting in the novel is that the physical amenities of the place soon wears off in people's minds, but they cling to it desperately because it irons out human differences between them. They cling to a homogeneous life, and both unhappy and alone and yet desiring to be in this place, and their lives unfold.

Madame Rochefort uses a word that seems to offer a clue as to why in general people would prefer to be with their own kind. She uses the word *happiness*, but she uses the word ironically. It's the desire for happiness that produces misery, and yet people cling to that precondition of equality and withdrawal from the unlike. Let me give you an American example of this irony. I wrote a book about ten years ago called *The Hidden Injuries of Class* with Jonathan Cobb. It's mostly about South Boston and white working-class families in Boston. In the course of the research I got to know some of these families quite well. After I finished writing the book, in the wake of one of the school riots in South Boston, I talked in 1974 to the father of one of the white boys who'd been involved and who'd been quite violent. He said to me, "I'm with my boy on this. You have to get the n-[*expletive*] out of here so that we can lead our own lives. Go back to the way it was." This was fantasy. The man speaking had grown up in Roxbury, which during the time he grew up had a large Black and Portuguese community, and his best friend was somebody he once described to me as "sort of Black"—that is, very dark Portuguese. I thought at the time that he was just protecting his child. Six months later I met him again at a bar in South Boston, and I asked him, about the expulsion of Black people, "Is it better?" And he said to me, "Well they're gone but it's funny, they're gone and we got no peace. I thought when there was nobody but people like us that we'd be happy, but we got no peace." And then I said to him, "Do you think that maybe, you know, you should change you attitudes about busing?" He said, "Oh no. No, no, that was the right thing to do."

It's that contradiction in consciousness that Madame Rochefort is getting at. This fantasy that somehow if you get rid of the stranger, if you exclude otherness, if everybody become homogeneous in that sense equal plane, then somehow some possibility of happiness, or in this case peace, would come. And yet, it isn't realized. It's what the Moral Majority is about. That is, it's about the destruction of difference and the destruction of otherness as a precondition of creating what they consider to be the conditions for familial happiness and morality. If gay people are forced back into the closet, if women lose control of their bodies, if nobody is allowed to be different, then the condition for this fantasy of the happy family will appear. Listening to them talk, it seems that somehow the fantasies of expulsion of difference and the notion of happiness are the same. We know rationally that putting people in jail for their sexuality is not an answer to one's own marital problems, but irrationality links them: that by expelling the other, by creating equality, by being alone in that sense, only with people like yourself, then somehow some state of happiness will come into being.

So now we've now identified in a rather rough intuitive way two elements of the social puzzle. Equality, in the sense of homogenization, creates feelings of solitude. Equality and withdrawal from the other seems a precondition of happiness that in fact creates no happiness but more emotional distress. And the question we have to ask ourselves is why people cling to the first element in this puzzle if the second element— the promise—does not yield its rewards. ——— This puzzle is what Alexis de Tocqueville, writing 150 years ago, perceived in germ, tried to explain in terms of the nature of democracy itself. In the second part of this talk I'm going to present his theory, and then in the third apply it to modern city life. Let me just tell you a little about the circumstances of this book because they're quite important. Tocqueville came from a minor family which was called *noblesse de la robe*, or court nobles, in France. In 1830, the Bourbon Restoration monarchy fell. People like Tocqueville's family, who were not of the people, withdrew into something called *emigration intérieur*, or inner withdrawal. Tocqueville, a twenty-six-year-old man, didn't want to do that, and he convinced the government to let him, with his friend Gustav de Beaumont, come to America and inspect prisons. Although he did write about prisons a bit, what he really wanted to do was understand the society of America, where everybody seemed to be mostly alike: this equality was an image of what Europe would be like in the future.

He made this trip in the 1830s and then went back to France and published the first volume of *Democracy in America*. And it was a bestseller. He waited five years to publish the second volume, and in those five years he had a lot of time to understand the new regime in France—the Orleanist Monarchy was also dedicated to a kind of bourgeois equality; not equality in the American sense, but bourgeois equality. There's a shift between these two volumes that is terribly important, and that shift is toward understanding our own present-day condition.

I want to start off in explaining Tocqueville's theory by telling you about a revolutionary discovery he made: the discovery of how to link up the sociology of equality with the politics of democracy. You know, via Robert's Rules of Order about fairness in the presentation of an argument—a notion which was still rather new wherein you debated an argument before you took the vote—and so on. He connected all of what could be called the mechanics of fairness to the social conditions of equality. He did so by defining equality as equality of condition, not opportunity. He wanted to understand America, our America, as a society in which people wanted to be more and more like each other—not alike at the start of a road race, where some people would come out different than others, but a society in which people wanted everyone to live the same way. What Tocqueville saw in America was a vision of a future Western world, in which the realization of personal desire encountered no checks by virtue of the existence of impersonal hierarchy. What is powerful in his vision is that he saw therefore that other kinds of checks to desire, and deformation of desire, would result precisely because there were no hierarchical hurdles to overcome. You take away the barrier because you are only a serf—everybody is the same, and what happens is that that very process is deforming. There's an untranslatable word in French that conveys this idea of equality: equality is a matter of *moeurs*—a style of behavior, I suppose, or morals understood in a social way—and upon the *moeurs* of equality are the political structures of society built.

Now these structures have a certain sequential pattern. I was told that I shouldn't go into all this because you're architects. However. You have to understand the structure. From the *moeurs* of equality, the people first derive the principle of legitimacy. Majority's rule is legitimate. Because if all the people are roughly the same in condition, then what the largest number of equals want will constitute a legitimate desire. From equality comes legitimacy. Tocqueville stresses again and again the derivation of legitimacy from egalitarian *moeurs* because he wants to explain how the conviction of a natural right grows up in people's minds. Natural right grows up not because people apprehend a fundamental truth of nature. The Enlightenment rhetoric about natural right in America is, according to Tocqueville, a terrible sociological illusion of the founding fathers. People don't believe in natural rights; they believe that you only have a natural right when you're all the same. Each man recognizes himself in all the others. The stronger the sense of recognition, the more natural the whole. The more I recognize myself to be like Moshe [Safdie], the more the sense of Us is charged with being the natural way to be. That's the conversion. And this equality is disguised as a natural right to majority rule.

By *democratic*, Tocqueville usually means the exercising of the vote in Parliamentary situations, in voluntary organization in New England town meetings, and so forth. This voting machinery always bring issues to a test. The rhythm of collective action is highly formalistic. No spontaneously felt general will is spontaneously acted upon, as it is for Jean-Jacques Rousseau. Reality must always be judged, measured, and defined through a mechanistic ritual of counting heads. Do you remember that we talked about Aristotle's idea of democracy at the end of the last talk? We talked about the necessity of a place where decision-making was something that could be arrived at spontaneously by direct discourse. Tocqueville redefines all of that. He says no, in a democracy, that's too anxiety-provoking. People want it mechanized; they want to make a technology of democracy, so that they can confirm to themselves that they all feel the same thing. They need to produce a sign world, a world of tangible symbols that are very mechanically arrived at, so that everybody can recognize that everybody else thinks the same thing. Whereas in spontaneous discourse you've got too many open parameters. It is a theory of the mechanization of democracy. And that's the flow of force in Tocqueville's thought, from equality to a principle of legitimacy to an illusion of natural law to democratic procedures for the majority to express its will. That's the quadrilogy. And the flow won't reverse. You can't start with a principle of political procedure, arrive at a principle of legitimacy, and from that create principles of equalization in society, which is what we tried to do in the 1960s.

Tocqueville often uses the words *democracy* and *equality* interchangeably. But the intent to separate them appeared, even in the preparatory work for *Democracy in America*, such as in a very interesting essay on religion in America, which Tocqueville wrote as he and Beaumont travelled from Manhattan to Niagara Falls. God knows why Niagara Falls stimulated him to this essay, but he always wrote about Niagara Falls. The sense of the matter is as follows: "That levelling in society and equality of condition is a force that has created politics that is far beyond the power of politics subsequently to control." I've spent a lot of time on this because we're now ready to look at Tocqueville's answer to our puzzle. Why do people in an egalitarian society with democratic procedures fear different ideas, people unlike themselves, and new experiences that might make them different? We've now arrived at the point of understanding how he's going to answer that question. There are two answers. One he gave in the first volume of *Democracy*, and one he gave in the second. The first of them deals with the tyranny of the majority, and the second deals with voluntary slavery.

In Volume One, Tocqueville said that because people believed there was an equality of condition in *moeurs* and believed in sentiments and feelings, that a democratic majority didn't simply take decisions, but they attempted to universalize them. And that leads to tyranny of the majority. The majority is not just content to say, well fifty-one percent of us has decided this, and you damn well better go along with it. Once that decision is taken, repressive pressure is put on the forty-nine percent who disagree to change not only their behavior but their beliefs, and to submit to that majority, to surrender themselves, and that difference of disagreement must disappear after the decision is taken. Everyone participates on an equal footing in society, and there is no real boundary between public life and private affairs. When therefore a sentiment is shared by a majority of the people so that they feel as one person, the particular person who might have a contrary opinion or sentiment feels an immense pressure from this majority. By what right does he or she dissent? What makes them feel so superior that they do not share the feelings of these equals? Now, they know through this technology of democracy what they believe. And this peer pressure, Tocqueville thought, either gradually seduces them into abandoning their position or forces them into exile. They are unlike the others and they do not belong—otherwise, they would feel as the others do.

Today we've got all sorts of names for the seduction that he's talking about in Volume One of *Democracy*: *self criticism*, *thought reform*, and the like. Tocqueville describes it as the spirit of courtiers extended to the whole character of society. People assure each other that they belong by mouthing similar thoughts. Equality of condition is ideologically confirmed by similarity of thought. Tocqueville cannot really explain why a majority needs to confirm itself through universalizing its decisions. He asserts that it occurs, and that the tyranny of the majority is the universalization of the *moeurs*, but he doesn't tell us why. And he knew it. He was very honest, unlike academic social philosophers, about the fact that his position was very fractured. It preyed on his mind after he finished the first volume of *Democracy*, and he took it up again after five years of seeing a kind of bourgeois egalitarianism in France. And, ultimately, in expanding the concept of the need of an egalitarian majority to absorb or expel a minority, he formulated a whole new notion of the dangers of egalitarian society. In the second volume he takes up the relationship between unhappiness and fear of others. I want to spend a lot of time on that connection. Settle in.

Perhaps the greatest writer on mass voluntary servitude before Tocqueville was Étienne de La Boétie, a sixteenth-century French writer who wrote a *Discours de la servitude volontaire*, or *Discourse on Voluntary Servitude*. The following passage puts his argument in a nutshell.

> So many men, so many villages, so many cities, so many nations, sometimes suffer under a single tyrant who has no other power than the power they give him; who could do them absolutely no injury unless they prefer to put up with him rather than contradict him. It is therefore the inhabitants themselves who permit, or rather who bring about their own subjection, since by ceasing to submit they would put an end to their servitude. A people enslaves itself, cuts its throat, gives consent to its own misery, or rather apparently welcomes it. It is the stupid and cowardly who are neither able to endure hardship nor to vindicate their rights; they stop at merely longing for them and lose through timidity the valor raised by the effort to claim these rights, although the desire to be free still remains as a part of their nature, a dream which echoes at night.

La Boétie moralizes voluntary slavery: although such slavery is a collective phenomenon, it results from the failures of personal character. The desire to be a slave results from a desire for comfort, and comfort induces the loss of will. Whereas, by the end of the second volume of *Democracy*, Tocqueville had come to conceive of voluntary slavery as a matter of personal discomfort and anxiety mediated by a peculiar set of social institutions. Personal discontent in an egalitarian society produces a sense of disconnection from public life, a loss of interest in all that lay outside the traumas of the self, and therefore a willingness to be ruled politically by an authoritarian regime. Tocqueville replaced La Boétie's indictment of voluntary slavery as moral failure with a notion of voluntary slavery as a kind of personal tragedy. It's an anxiety about individuals, about their individual worth, correlated to a loss of interest in social matters, which can't be brought within the circle of self-validation. "The more we're alike, what am I worth?" Society renders people passive in social terms by making them focus more and more on themselves, unsure of their value as individuals. The equation between private misery and public apathy is what's profound about this theory.

The curtain opens on this tragedy in the first chapter in the second part of Volume Two. It begins with what we call today a treatise in social psychology. In Volume One, Tocqueville had declared the primacy of the social experience of equality over political experience. He says, "Equality can establish itself in society and yet be absent in the political world." By that he meant religious equality without political freedom. When I read the newspapers about Iran I keep thinking about Tocqueville, because it is the kind of situation he had in mind. Now, in Volume Two, Tocqueville pursues the possibility that the desire for social equality actually weakens the desire for political liberty. Why? Is there some reason that the stronger the desire for social equality should weaken the desire for political liberty? The rest of Volume Two is largely devoted to answering this question in a different way than Volume One.

To love liberty, and to seek it out, requires a person to take risks. The desire for social equality is born out of a contrary impulse: the desire for immediate gratification, tangible gratification, above all in family relations. There's no accident about modern movements like the Moral Majority Tocqueville previewed. The family seems to be what is under attack, because that is the mediating institution for equality. People cherish the illusion that once they're on a plane with everyone else, then they'll have a security that will allow them to enjoy the "sweet pleasures of everyday existence," while liberty demands the renunciation of these pleasures. It's because of parenting and coupling that people are more ardent in their desire for equality than in their desire for liberty.

Having set up this imbalance, Tocqueville is ready to show how the pursuit of a peaceful *vie quotidien*, or everyday life, gradually leads people to a state of anxiety, unrest, and pleasurelessness. That is, they imagine that they could, by sacrificing their liberties, gain pleasure, when in fact they don't. And the very fact they don't gain it reinforces the desire for more equality. Tocqueville explains this by coining a new word: *individualism*. Tocqueville declares that this condition is a unique modern historical production. He brings forth the character of modern individualism by contrasting it to egoism. He defines egoism as a passionate and exaggerated love of oneself, and it leads a person to relate everything to himself and to prefer his own needs to everything else, which I think would be a very good definition of Emerson in the kind of passage that I first read to you in this lecture. Individualism is unhappy individuals as defined by contrast as "a peaceful and moderated feeling, which leaves each citizen to isolate himself from the mass of his equals, and to withdraw to within the circle of his family and their friends. Further having created this little society for his immediate ease, he willingly abandons the large society to go its own way."

It's often said that the nineteenth century was the era of individualism, both in ideology and in practice. This cliche does great violence to Tocqueville's use of the word. He's not using it in the sense that the social Darwinists would come to use it. His individualism is not a world of rugged struggle for survival, agonistic and hard, but exactly the reverse. Or, think of the differences between Jacob Burkhardt's use of individualism to describe the modern spirit born in the Italian Renaissance cities and Tocqueville's usage. Burkhardt shows us men and women struggling to win praise from one another. Struggling to be recognized as individuals because they have special outstanding qualities. This display of *virtús* is anarchic, but it involves a strong sense of community; in other words, you've got to want other people's praise, and to want other people's praise you've got to interact with them and you've got to be with them.

Tocqueville shows us men and women who no longer make demands on each other, save the demand to be left alone. His individuals do not want praise for being extraordinary, they want to be just like everybody else, sort of good ordinary Joes, so that nobody will give them any trouble and they can, in modern argot, do their own thing. Now, paradoxically this individualism arises only because a certain kind of group life exists. Once the fantasy arises that equality of condition will give each person access to living peacefully—because it will stabilize the family—only then does the person desire to withdraw from his fellows to isolate himself. This personal desire to withdraw is, in other words, created by a collective life whose ideology is that social similarity holds out the promise that men will no longer have to delay gratifying their small-scale desires for comfort.

With this theory of individualism Tocqueville becomes a true social psychologist, but a paradoxical one. The emotion that modern collective life arouses is that a person can withdraw from collective life—everybody is pretty much like oneself, so that one need not worry about violation and disruption, therefore one leaves public affairs in the hands of the state and cultivates one's own garden.

I've used the word *fantasy* to describe the basis of this individualism because it identifies Tocqueville's view of the relation of this collective psychology to collective reality in an egalitarian society. In fact, the practice of individualism does not lead to the result of intimate small-scale gratification. Withdrawal from association with other people creates instead a ceaseless striving after pleasure. One attempts to gorge oneself on the experiences that are available to everyone because everyone's on an equal footing of action. You are an incomplete human being. This is the logic of advertising: there's something that someone else has which you could have. There is no barrier; the sky's the limit. You can thus be manipulated by ideological instruments of advertising so that you feel that what you have right now is never enough. Possession loses its meaning. That's the most important thing about this theory. This psychology is an attempt to explain why Americans are not like the French bourgeois, who love every franc and centime of their possessions. Americans in Tocqueville's scheme don't really have a sense of the pleasure of owning, but they have a sense of the pleasure of acquisition. Is that clear? People can work for twenty years to have a house in New York and then decide to give it up and move to Florida because it is supposed to be better there—at least that's how it is advertised. The satisfaction of owning one's own house fades; the mobile individual starts over with a new mortgage. That sort of thing is, at a practical level, what Tocqueville is talking about.

Tocqueville created a theory of what could be called *horizontal restlessness*. The more that a society destroyed hierarchic barriers to action, the more the diversity of experience occurs within a single central band, then the more people believed that they must exhaustively explore all forms of living in order to be psychologically complete. What is, is never enough. Tocqueville contrasts this horizontal restlessness to the deprivations of an *ancien regime* village, by saying that those at the bottom of a hierarchy, in a hierarchical world, enjoy what is available to them while at the same time resenting the evils they presently endure. On the contrary, the citizens of an egalitarian society discount the reality of their present condition and think only of the events and gratifications they have yet to enjoy, independently of whatever a person experiences at a given moment. This is a great quote from Tocqueville: "He imagines a thousand other gratifications which death will keep him from knowing, if he does not hurry. This thought troubles him, fills him with fear and regret, and maintains his spirit in a state of incessant trepidation. At every moment he feels he is on the verge of changing his designs and his place in life. It is exactly in egalitarian society that will arouse this restlessness," he argues. "Neither law nor custom, pins a person down to a place. The concept of external necessity disappears and is replaced by the demands of a more internalized sort. Out of fear of being deprived, where nothing social and hierarchic stands in the way of possible gratification, whatever one's current condition, everything becomes by definition not enough."

This anxiety shapes the culture of ambition. People are ceaselessly ambitious but the scope of their ambition is petty, and this narrowing occurs for two reasons. First, ambition that is possible to harbor in an egalitarian society can't be grand in scope, and it cannot aim at domination of others, for this would so upset the others that the majority would move inexorably to bring the strong man down. Exceptional power must be hidden, Tocqueville says. It must be mystified. Thus you get somebody like Ronald Reagan, who is the representative for vast, vast amounts of cash and interest, making himself out to be a good ordinary Joe; he always has to hide his real power by pretending he's just an ordinary man. Who just happens to know these people who have these vast sums of money. But let's not talk about that. Ambition has to be hidden if it's large, and those who are capable of large things must dissemble—whether they're capable of great evil or great good, they must dissemble. The man similarly possessed of an idea, a project, is a man unlike others; he doesn't fit in. And society so treats its members that fewer and fewer are willing to appear as pariahs.

This formula has ethnic consequence, apparent in our time. In the late 1960s and early 1970s, when there were discussions about integrating Black people into the fabric of New York City, one constantly heard this would come through creating a new middle class. I remember sitting through these meetings during which people talk about how we can create a Black bourgeois in New York, and wondered whether this meant that the people who can't be made bourgeois are therefore less legitimate. That kind of pressure is what Tocqueville has in mind. Somebody who is not digestible as normal appeals as somebody who therefore should not enjoy the same rights. You acquire more rights the more you can be digested into something where other people can recognize you as like them.

What does it mean that ambitions become smaller in order that they might be more easily recognized? Tocqueville saw two political consequences coming from democratic restlessness combined with restricted ambition. Resistance to state and the will to fight for liberty diminishes, clearly. The demand for liberty doesn't easily mesh with the social and consumer ambitions individuals in an equal society harbor. Moreover, political action seems to be a shaming of others, who are simply trying to find and make a life for themselves, to engage in self-discovery through increasingly trivial forms of experience. Why is this person asking us to sacrifice ourselves for a far-off goal? The search for liberty becomes an insult to others who are not searching. They have retreated into a private yearning. They say it doesn't matter, forget all of that. What makes you think you're so special?

And what is true of dissent applies to broader social difference. There is something insulting about having to deal with people who have no desire to become like you, but instead confront you. The whole schema of equality of condition legitimating personal withdrawal is called into question. You can become *sur motive*, overmotivated in your anger. Because it isn't just that their way of life is different than yours, but it's also the fact that you can never become like them. That is the kind of provocation that in democracies makes discourse with the others so painful. If I could put it another way, people who are intractably other—like poor Black people, or Jews who have no desire to act like Christians—somebody who is intractably other calls into account the notion that an individual has chosen to be the kind of person she or he is. That makes an individual even more anxious, and one way to diminish anxiety is to desensitize oneself, denying that the other has an independent existence. "I only recognize real when it's what's like me."

Tocqueville's analyses of ambition and egalitarian passion were the origin of the pressure we speak today of pressures for conformity. His conclusion was that they arise not as the smugness of those seeking to make others conform, but out of the very need to validate the meaning of their individual frustration in the sense that nothing is ever enough. That's why discourse with somebody who is intractably different becomes the ultimate threat. It opens the door to ever-greater existential anxiety. A terrible vista of feeling incomplete. I want to read you one more quote from Tocqueville. This is my translation, so you'll have to forgive me.

> I see a vast crowd of people similar and equal who revolve without repose around themselves, in pursuit of petty and vulgar pleasures, pleasures from which they hope to fill up their souls. Each person, withdrawn into himself, behaves as though he is a stranger to the destiny of others. And those who are strangers he sees as having no destiny akin to his own. His children and his good friends constitute for him the whole of the human species, as for his transactions with his fellow citizens, he may mix among them, but he sees them not, he touches them but does not feel them, he exists only in himself and for himself alone. And if on these terms there remains a sense in his mind of family, there is no longer a sense of society.

Here in sum is a theoretical definition of democracy founded on equality radically at odds with the kind of Aristotlean definition we were working at in the last lecture about democracy founded on discourse with the other. ——— Now, I move to the third part of my long-winded lecture. What relation does this theory have to modern city life? I'm going to answer this rather briefly. ——— Consider for a moment Jane Jacobs's ideal city. Everything that Jane Jacobs sees as making city life vibrant Tocqueville would see as setting in motion the democratic impulse to destroy the other. I'll isolate three elements from *The Life and Death of Great American Cities*. First, her belief that in cities there should be intermixture without integration. Second, her belief in informal street control through spontaneous surveillance. And third, her belief that bringing together social classes accomplishes a kind of social peace in cities. I happen to believe all these things, by the way, but we have to understand the difficulty of asserting these beliefs.

Let's look at these three things. First, the doctrine of intermixture without integration. That means you live in a city in which people are constantly experiencing differences. For instance, I live near Little Italy and Chinatown; the kind of openness to each other that Jane is talking about just doesn't happen, even though we mix in the street. We're intermixed but we don't speak. Obviously I can't become Chinese. Tocqueville's explanation for this silence that the bonds of community among people are so fragile, so anxiety-laden, that people withdraw into themselves. Dense, diverse cities prompt that withdrawal. When urbanites are face-to-face with people who simply cannot be integrated into their world, they're provoked to evermore anxiety about themselves. My students in New York have been gathering data for the last eight years, about why people resist living in racially integrated neighborhoods, which pretty much seems to bear this Tocquevillian point out. Such people may be racist, or not, but regardless what's more important is the fact that they feel anxious about living with differences, anxious about the experience of complexity. In other words, Tocqueville would say Jane Jacobs's idea of intermixture without integration is a recipe for absolute anxiety about oneself and therefore rejection of others. Mutual silence rules.

Let's take a look at the second aspect of what Jane proposes. That is informal social control on the streets through various spontaneous means. Her views are akin to Oscar Newman's work on defensible space. Unlike them, Tocqueville asserts that the spontaneous tools of control are not how equal indvidiauls operate. Go back to the very beginning of what he was talking about, the nineteenth-century version of Robert's Rules of Order. What people want are mechanical means of ratification of what their rules are. The notion of a spontaneous rule, or of a kind of a shifting, quasi-anarchic give-and-take of street surveillance, would be highly disturbing as it requires too much effort. Therefore people feel that spontaneous control is no control at all. Now, for those of you who have grown outside of New York or in other diverse places, the trouble is that they see chaos and anarchy in the city. That's what Tocqueville is trying to explain—that in a society dominated by democratic ideology, people feel constantly anxious. Only rigid rules guarantee that they can be left alone in peace. That is, a transformation of the egalitarian impulse into the bureaucracy of power.

The third urban principle of Jane Jacobs is to bring together social classes. I'm not talking about people of different races or ethnicities, but about people who could share something but do not share social class. This principle raises a profoundly interesting problem about Tocqueville, just because we don't live in an equal society of economic conditions. In his time, Jacksonian America was a fairly equal economic society—I mean, the percentage of the population that were free landholders was staggering. We don't live in that society, instead in a very unequal, class-articulated society. Yet everything we read in this second volume resonates. And there's a conundrum here. I'll try to put it as follows. Tocqueville's legacy is to explain why an ideology of equality, of *moeurs*, of individual withdrawal, is strengthened by the experience of class differentiation. The more class differentiation we have in America, the stronger the ideology of equality becomes. Thus if the prime goal in urban housing is to mix social classes together, the result will be a dead community, people withdrawn into themselves, as Tocqueville puts it. I'm just going to leave this as a proposition, and for those of you who are free we can judge its correctness tomorrow. This proposition is a profound challenge to Jane Jacobs or my book *Uses of Disorder*. The diverse open city, which people like Jane Jacobs and myself believe in, is unbearable.

So, this is our conundrum in these first two lectures. Egalitarian democracy versus the democratic city. And two very, very different notions of what democracy means: one based on discourse and could be among unequals, and one based on equals. Now, I've said nothing in this exposition about the visual aspect and the visual consequences of this theory, but you see two immediate problems that we'll take up in the next lecture. How can the visual environment heighten anxiety about strangers, those who are different, or outsiders? And secondly, how can the visual environment desensitize people out of the kind of anxieties that Tocqueville is talking about?

In the next lecture, the lecture on Aesthetics of Isolation, for which we'll have slides, if I can ever figure out how to do them, I want to show—and I'll be using only examples from Paris and New York that I took this fall—how modern architects and planners have unwittingly acted out this Tocquevillian tragedy. So that, on the one hand, they've heightened anxiety when they tried to create visual diversity of a certain type, and much more importantly that they've engaged in a kind of aesthetics of desensitization to the environment, because that's what this whole Tocquevillian analysis is about. You must desensitize yourself to the environment in order to feel free to pursue this kind of inner drama within yourself. And could I ask, since I'm going to talk about a theory of urban desensitization, that you read an article by Georg Simmel called "The Metropolis and Mental Life"? Fortunately, you can read it in a book I edited called *Classic Essays on the Culture of Cities*. It also appears in *The Sociology of Georg Simmel*, although my book will earn me lots of cash if you buy it. Or you can get it out of the library. But we've set up the terms of the first two lectures and where we're going is a kind of terrible conundrum. How can we have democracy in cities? And what kind of democracy is it that we mean? Next time we're going to look at the ways in which the experience of our eyes bears on the condition of the encounter with otherness, and on the other side, this Tocquevillian problem that the encounter with otherness may be terribly anxiety-provoking, and that in fact what people want is to have an environment that is humanly desensitizing. So, that is how the flow to the next lecture will occur. Thank you.

THE CIVILIZED MODERN CITY

RICHARD: Today I want to speak to you about what it means to call a modern city *civilized*. What makes the modern city not simply a place to live and work in, but a place in which to develop as a human being as one might not in a small town or in a countryside? In the course of this lecture, I hope to connect some ideas about urban civilization to the political concerns about democracy that have appeared in previous lectures. ——— A medieval German saying expresses one idea of the civilization of a city. *Stadt Luft macht frei* means that "city air makes men free." In the medieval German city this saying conveyed that people were free from the obligations of feudalism if they lived in a city for more than a year and a day. They were free for *bürgerliche Gesellschaft*, which meant "a life conducted in the city, according to the individual's capacities." Usually that conduct in life in the economic sphere involved commerce. But more generally and deeply, this *bürgerliche Gesellschaft* meant that a person participated in an urban society whose rules the participant helped make. Man obeys in the city not because of inherited tradition, not because of feudal code, but because he has formed the very laws he obeys.

This is why we find so often in Hanseatic and other German medieval and urban documents the association of the social description *bürgerliche Gesellschaft*, with a philosophical ideal of *Wirklichkeit*, which means in German what it means in English: of actuality, of being here now, of not simply passing through life, but living it. This conjunction of freedom and *aktualität* in the medieval city is why, to Max Weber, this period of urban history represented the summit of what the term *urban civilization* implies. It isn't just that people are free from feudal obligations; urban freedom changed how people experienced time. In cities lay the birth of historical consciousness. Historians like Isaiah Berlin assert that the consciousness of historical time occurs with Giambattista Vico in the eighteenth century. Not at all. In everyday life, the notion of freedom, joined to the peculiar character of time, of *aktualität*, defined the civilization of a medieval city.

Max Weber thought that the great industrial cities of the twentieth century represented an opposite condition. A barbaric urban culture, as size, density, and capitalism put an end to living now, freely. Weber was certainly not alone in bemoaning the loss of the medieval world. I'd like to recall to you a famous passage from *The Communist Manifesto*:

> The bourgeoisie has put an end to all feudal, patriarchal, idyllic relations. It has pitilessly torn asunder, and has left no other bond between man and man than naked self-interest, than callous cash payment. It has drowned the most heavenly ecstasies of religious fervor, of chivalrous enthusiasm, of philistine sen-timentalism, in the icy water of egotistical calculation.

More:

> The bourgeoisie has stripped of its halo every occupation hitherto honored and looked up to with reverent awe. It has torn away from the family its sentimental veil.

The modern city has thus served as a kind of focus to such feelings of regret, usually in contrast to this all but vanished medieval past, both in social theory and ordinary opinion. In reading the city there is a tendency to view it symbolically as a landscape of loss, as wasteland in contrast to the civilized medieval city. ——— The argument I want to make today is that this imagery of a modern urban wasteland misses the possibilities of modern city life. Just as the medieval burgher class was set free from feudalism in the city, I believe the modern city offers another kind of freedom: the freedom from what Émile Durkheim called *organic solidarity*. Just as the capacity of medieval man to make the laws that he obeyed gave him a new sense of time, a sense of *aktualität*, freedom in the modern city can give us a life of presence, presentness, actuality, and nowness. This actual freedom is not a condition experienced routinely in the city, rather it is a possibility of city life that occasionally becomes real for us, catches us unawares, and so often frightens us that we dream of going back into the womb of life on Tocqueville's suffocating terms.

In talking about championing this possible, occasionally experienced urban actuality, I don't mean to do so as something that gives pleasure. What I want to describe is a kind of tragic liberty, which is possible for people in a modern city. But I believe that until we come to terms with this possible freedom, the possibility of democracy in the cities will elude us. ———— This lecture is in three parts. In the first I wish to describe the nature of this urban actuality. Or rather I shall explore one theory of it, which occurs in perhaps the greatest single essay on the culture of the modern city: Georg Simmel's "The Metropolis and Mental Life." Simmel's argument connects to Walter Benjamin's great work on Baudelaire in Paris, both in an essay called "On Some Motifs in Baudelaire," and in an essay called "Paris, Capital of the 19th Century." "On Some Motifs in Baudelaire" appears in a book called *Illuminations* in English, and for "Paris, Capital of the 19th Century" there's a good translation in the *New Left Review* from 1978 and an accessible but not so good translation in a collection of Benjamin's writings called *Reflections*.

In the second part of the talk, I want to briefly compare how Simmel's idea of an urban individual compares to Tocqueville's idea of a democratic individual, and so connect the last lecture to this one. And in the third part, I'd like us to consider what Simmel's theory implies about the possibility of democratic discourse. The whole point of this lecture is to lead you, and myself as well, up to something that is very unsatisfying: an irreconcilable conflict of values. It exists between the peculiar freedom that is possible in the city, this *aktualität*, and the value placed on exchange in democratic theory. There is a real conflict between a kind of free individuality in the city in the very best sense, and the foundation of democratic theory—that is, the value put on discourse.

As a preface to talking about Simmel and Benjamin, I thought to start by describing a community that I both lived in for a long time and am now studying. You know about this community because of Jane Jacobs celebrating it in *The Death and Life of Great American Cities*. It's the far West Village in Manhattan. She celebrated it as an ideal of free, complex, vibrant urban community. I moved into this community just around the time she was writing the book, with two other people into a one-room apartment at West 10th Street and West Street right near the docks on the West Side Highway. Three of us living in one room—all chastely, unfortunately. It was over a bar called Dirty Dick's Fo'c'sle Bar, which we had little contact with for the first week we lived there, until one of us ran out of cigarettes and we went downstairs to investigate; the place turned out to be New York's greatest transvestite bar. Dirty Dick's Fo'c'sle Bar was next to a Tabernacle church, both were across the street from a big shipping company run by Italians.

Image of West Street, looking north from Christopher Street, where Dirty Dick's Fo'c'sle Bar was located. The photo is from the late 1970s, sometime after the bar closed, and was taken from the West Side Highway, which was an elevated highway before it was dismantled in 1989.

THE INCIDENTS

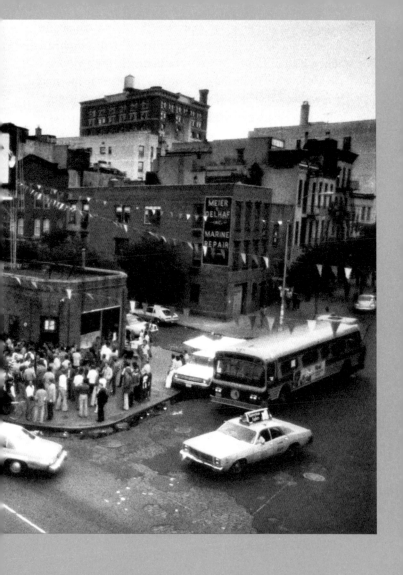

Next to the Italian shipping company was the central supply for all Chinese groceries in the city. So, a diverse and complicated community. Rather funny, as well. For instance, the action in Dirty Dick's Fo'c'sle Bar heated up around three in the morning, just when we were trying to sleep, and usually tailed off about eight in the morning when the truckers would just be starting to deliver their goods. The truckers and the transvestites from Dirty Dick's would go up the street to a coffee shop, and it was quite a scene at eight in the morning: men who were quite blasted out from nights of whatever and truckers who were just about to go to work. They cohabitated, Jane Jacobs describes, in harmony, even a kind of mutual toleration. The Chinese people couldn't make heads or tails of any of this, and I don't blame them. They drank silently and suspiciously. ——— The neighborhood in the last fifteen years has evolved into a much more simple community, and a student of mine, Martin Levine, and I are trying to study what's happened. Basically it has become a gay ghetto, changing in four ways.

Time segregation has appeared in the community; that is to say, different kinds of people use it at different times. There's still a warehouse district, but the warehouses have begun making deliveries early at night and don't seem to make deliveries early in the morning. The gay people who live in the community are not quite as exuberant as the people at Dirty Dick's and they seem to disappear before the commerce of the bars really begins. The people who work in the community in the middle of the day leave it at night. There has arisen an office part of the West Village, delivering office supplies to the city, and those people are absolutely absent when not at work.

The reason this time segregation has occurred is the second change from what Jane Jacobs dealt with—that is, there has been a kind of ghettoization, if you'll pardon the word, through gentrification. The old warehouses are declining, now taken over by developers who transform them into studios and one-bedroom apartments where lots of gay guys live. The residential community has gradually become more expansive as the community gets "better." The third thing that's happened is a new relationship to the police, wherein the old adversarial relationship is gone and the police now serve a very protective function for the bourgeois gay community. Still, there's lots of harassment. Outside my door a couple of years ago two men were killed, and crazed Moral Majority types occasionally appear in gangs and harass people in the community. So, in addition to the kind of ghettoed gentrification, there's a slight siege mentality about the West Village, overlaid with a vast quantity of tourists who come to see what's going on. Finally, the community has attempted to create a certain kind of barrier for itself, in that the more middle-class gay people in the community want to prevent it from becoming a kind of gay Times Square by reducing the number of porn shops and all-night clubs.

So, with that description that Jane Jacobs has made of the West Village, the community has moved on beyond that to become something more simple and monodimensional. Still the people who live here believe they have a freedom in the city now that was not possible before in their lives, and which they could have nowhere else in the country. In this half-ghetto, the question is, what kind of freedom, and how much freedom? Simmel's essay helps elucidate the issues involved assessing what it means for people to be free in such a community.

The essay developed out of a lecture that Simmel gave in the 1890s, during a time when anti-Semitism in Germany, particularly in Berlin, was on the ascent. The subtext of his lecture is how the city might be a protection for deviants like Jews. In what way could one take the development of the modern city as a place where Jews, like gay people eighty years later, might feel a sense of protection because of the social construction of the city itself? That's not a task he addresses directly, as I say it's subtext. He wants to show something much grander. He wants to show how individuality is developed when people are caught in certain kinds of social tensions. How *Geistesleben*, spiritual life, is neither the mechanical reflection of material life, as the kind of vulgar Marxists believe, and not divorced from matters of spirit, as the traditional kind of problem in German philosophy. People become distinctive spirits, Simmel argued, from the way in which they cope with social opposites, tensions, or contradictions not of their own making. In this essay Simmel defined those tensions that characterize the modern city, out of which an individual might be developed. The basic tension of urban culture is the tension between psychic overstimulation versus defensive desensitization—these are dreadful English translations, but the ideas they represent are very simple. "The psychological basis of the city," Simmel says, is "the intensification of nervous stimulation which results from the swift and uninterrupted change of outer and inner stimuli, the swift and uninterrupted alternation"—that might be a better translation, of "outer and inner stimuli."

He explains this as follows. Here is a passage from the opening of the essay.

> Man is a differentiating creature. His mind is stimulated by the difference between a momentary impression and the one which preceded it. Lasting impressions, impressions which differ only slightly from one another, impressions which take a regular and habitual course and show regular and habitual contrasts—all of these use up, so to speak, less consciousness than does the rapid crowding of changing images, the sharp discontinuity in the grasp of a single glance, and the unexpectedness of onrushing impressions. These are the psychological conditions which the metropolis creates. With each crossing of the street, with the tempo and multiplicity of economic, occupational, and social life, the city sets up a deep contrast with small town and rural life with reference to the sensory foundations of the psyche. What this metropolis exacts from man as a discriminating creature is a different kind of consciousness from rural life.

This is his basic supposition. That the essential condition of the city is a kind of stimulation that is rapid, sharp, and discontinuous. Now, if a person yielded himself up to this stimulation then he or she would go mad, so as a defense, as an effort of sanity, the person looks for ways to desensitize his or her own perceptions. And finds a way through the defensive uses of intellect. Simmel says:

> The intellect is the most adaptable of our inner
> forces. In order to accommodate to change
> and to the contrast of phenomena, the intellect
> does not require any shocks or inner upheavals
> [...]. The metropolitan type of man, which
> of course exists in a thousand individual vari-
> ants, develops an organ protecting him against
> the threatening currents and discrepancies of
> his external environment, which would uproot
> him. He reacts with his head rather than his
> heart. In this, an increased awareness assumes
> the psychic prerogative. Metropolitan life,
> thus, underlies a heightened awareness and a
> predominance of intelligence in metropolitan
> man [...]. Intellectuality is thus seen to pre-
> serve subjective life against the overwhelming
> power of metropolitan life.

Similarly, Freud writes:

> The acceptance of shocks is facilitated by
> training in coping with stimuli and, if need be,
> dreams as well as recollection may be enlisted.
> As a rule, however this training devolves upon
> the wakeful consciousness, located in a part
> of the cortex which is "so blown out by the
> effect of the stimulus" that it offers the most
> favorable situation for the reception of stimuli.
> That the shock is thus cushioned, parried
> by consciousness, would lend the incident that
> occasions it the character of having been
> lived in the strict sense.

That is, it lends it actuality, or *aktualität*. ——— I know this
opposition between psychic overstimulation and the defense of
the desensitizing intellect seems like a commonplace resolved
by a cliche. "It's all too much" resolved by "I withdraw." I want
to redeem Simmel's idea of psychological shock resolved by
withdrawal and desensitization by comparing it to an account
of a similar problem analyzed by Walter Benjamin. It appears
when Benjamin describes the poet Baudelaire's relationship to
Paris, just to give you an idea of what Simmel is talking about.

What Benjamin wanted to do in this famous essay was show in the poet's work how the essential character of the city, its shock value, could stimulate poetic intelligence in the sense of creating a plan, a plan of perception. And Benjamin tells us exactly what Baudelaire's plan was. I will read you a long passage from him:

> The greater the share of the shock factor in particular impressions, the more constantly consciousness has to be alert as a screen against stimuli. The more efficiently it does so, the less these impressions enter experience, tending to remain in the sphere of a certain hour of one's life. Perhaps the special achievement of shock defense may be seen in its function of assigning to an incident a precise point in time in consciousness at the cost of the integrity of the stimuli. This would be a peak achievement of the intellect. It would turn the incident into a moment that has been lived. Without reflection there would be nothing but the sudden start, usually the sensation of fright which, according to Freud, confirms the failure of the shock defense. Baudelaire has portrayed this condition in a harsh image. He speaks of a duel in which the artist, just before being beaten, screams in fright. This duel is the creative process itself. Thus Baudelaire has placed the shock experience at the very center of his artistic work.

A poet to be willing to deform the integrity of sensory impressions, to, as he says, "assign an incident a precise point in time," and, second, to turn the incident into a moment that's been lived. What this means, as in all of Baudelaire's poems on the city, is that when Baudelaire says "I feel this," he assigns it a moment. And at that moment the sensation happens only then. There are no eternal moments of feeling, such as Keats evokes in his "Ode on a Grecian Urn." That is, the signs make his own sensory organization dependent upon time. There is no sense of "it's already happened to me." Rather than the retreat from feeling, which Simmel describes, for Benjamin or Baudelaire poetry opens up feelings at the the gateway to free consciousness of the city.

Against urban aesthetics Simmel has in fact argued very pithily. He says "an increased awareness assumes a psychic prerogative." That is, becoming aware becomes the way in which we defend against being stimulated, so that there's a tradeoff between stimulation and consciousness. I go into all of this because it is a foundation for a whole theory of liberty based on a person's sensory apparatus in the city. There's a tradeoff between sensation and consciousness. If you had just the sensation you'd be destroyed; on the other hand, that consciousness has a meaning only because it's responding to a stimulus that is dangerous, threatening, and strong. I said that for Simmel essentially the analysis of the structure of the city is the structure of connections, and they're all derived from this basic one between overstimulation and defensive intelligence. That is, he derives this to a conjunction between passivity in obeying orders and economic rationality, or what he calls *objectification*. I just want to focus on the basic one that has to do with the development of this individuality.

What is it that creates this relationship between shock and a deforming consciousness? Simmel doesn't really tell us, but we can easily deduce it. We know that urban complexity of all sorts—and people like Jane Jacobs and myself when I was in my youth celebrate it—create the shock. There's a famous saying by Raymond Hood that congestion is good. This was in reference to Rockefeller Center. By that he meant congestion creates stimulation. Simmel would likely have found this ridiculous. For Simmel, the material condition of urban life creates its culture: there are too many events and too many people on the street. As a result an individual consciousness is created. It's very important to understand exactly what this means. Individuality is not something you inalienably possess. It is a dependent function of the street. The more you're in a situation of street stimulation, the more individuality you will develop. This is a fundamental point of Simmel's sociology, and indeed of any understanding of what we mean by individualism. It's not given to you by God, and you don't possess individuality in Simmel's view because of your talents or your abilities you possess, but you develop individuality because you have submitted yourself to the play of dissonant forces. And that's why individuality develops in a city more than it develops in the countryside—because the play of tensions is greater and is orchestrated in another way.

Christmas light show, Rockefeller Center, New York City.

THE INCIDENTS

For people like myself who work in this Simmelian tradition, this sets us apart from romantics of the city, who bemoan the breakdown of organic life through this kind of tension Simmel has described. The people who don't regret it but see it as an opportunity in the city do so because that is the means by which an adult human being develops a personality, or, to put it in jargon, how you develop what I call a social individuality. I think we don't understand in city planning how to shape the material conditions of stimulation to encourage this individuality to develop, without withdrawal into the fantasy of community.

Why should a person submitted to tension of this sort in the city develop what I call this social individuality? Here is Simmel's explanation:

> On the one hand, life is made infinitely easy for the personality in that stimulations, interests, uses of time, and consciousness are offered to it from all sides in the city. They carry the person as if in a stream, and one hardly needs to swim for oneself. On the other hand, however, life is composed more and more of those impersonal contents and offerings which tend to displace the genuine personal colorations and incomparabilities. This results in the individual's summoning to the utmost what is ever unique and particular about him, in order to preserve a personal core whose content he has yet to experience. He has to exaggerate this personal element in order to remain audible even to himself.

Marvelous phrase, isn't it? But Simmel has to exaggerate this personal element in order to remain audible even to himself. That this atrophy of individual culture occurs through the hypertrophy of objective culture is one reason for the bitter hatred which the preachers of the most extreme individualism, above all Nietzsche, harbor against the metropolis. But it is indeed also a reason why these preachers are so passionately loved in the metropolis, and why they appear to the metropolitan man as the prophets and saviors of his most unsatisfied yearnings. —— Now, my version of what I would call this social individuality is that the attempt both to open oneself up to diversity and to defend against it through codes of deflecting meaning, as did Baudelaire, creates the desire to assert oneself as a distinctive person. It's a tremendous paradox. We started off with two perceptual modes, one in response to the other. Overstimulation, this kind of deformative defense. What this leads to is a definitional mode of oneself beyond either. That is, you don't opt for one of those modes over the other. What happens in that is a kind of assertion of oneself that goes beyond either. That is, a dialectics of development in the city. That, for me, at this point in my own thinking about the city, is what civilization represents: a dialectic of perception, which leads to the attempt to develop the self.

I'll furnish an example, from the study that Martin Levine and I are doing among the gay community in the West Village, of what this civility is about. I've been interviewing several men there who have been in the city for the last six or seven years. Most of them are in their mid-twenties, so coming just when they became adults. I'd like to describe one of them, who is now twenty-seven and came to New York when he was twenty-one. His first reaction to the city, and particularly the sexual freedom possible for gay people in New York, was for him to abandon himself. Bars, discos, etc.—a Fellini sexuality. It was absolutely unstinting. Lots of drugs, lots of casual encounters. And after a couple of years of this, he sought to make some order out of this chaos, by becoming highly demanding sexually. Interested only in a very particular kind of S/M which is only available in two clubs, rejecting all lovers who didn't fit his desires.

He said to me in one of these interviews, "I screened them out even when I wanted them, if they didn't fit this way I had of anchoring myself." For the sake of finding an anchor, there's a kind of screening process that goes on to deal with overstimulation. In another year the flux came back, and he was then caught for a period of about eighteen months passing, as he says, "from my screen to surrendering." About two years ago, a third element entered the picture, and it constitutes the element of a more durable individuality. It has to do with the violin. He said to me at one point, "You see, I played the violin as a child, but lost interest in it in college. But I needed something, something me, something that would mean simply that I did, that I made. I can't sort out cruising and screening, I've given up sorting it out, and I'm a terrible violinist. But somehow, practicing three hours a day, it lets me sort out this other thing."

That statement is the essence of what the dialectics of individuality is about. That the assertion of something that is oneself, that one asserts arbitrarily as oneself, is a way of creating a human being surmounts the tension of being too much stimulation and defensive screening out. It's not a resolution of the two, but it's a third way—it's a dialectic exactly in the way in which Hegel uses that term. That statement—"But somehow, practicing three hours a day, it lets me sort out this other thing"—is a dialectical evolution of personality. ——— Now, this evolution of a life in the city is what I mean by urban freedom. It's not the resolution of contradiction, but the isolating and magnifying of elements of oneself that permit one to live in conflict. And I think readers among you of Jacob Burkhardt see where this leads—that is, the individual as an assertion, or, in his terms, as a work of art.

So we've arrived at a rather abstract idea of what I think we mean by the term *urban civilization*, via this artificial reading of Simmel and Benjamin. Cities offer people the freedom to experience contradiction, and that the result of that will be the assertion of oneself, not in order to leave those contradictions, but in order to create something for oneself, of oneself. This is what's missing in works like Oscar Newman or Jane Jacobs— they don't describe the evolution of personality required to bear the cities that they imagine to be good because they are diverse. I believe it's out of that very dialectic between psychic over-stimulation and defense that a kind of individualism is created that possesses the quality of *aktualität*. One lives in the here and now. And I believe it's a freedom that all of us have in the city, which does not happen all at once.

Let me briefly conclude by comparing this kind of individualism to Tocqueville's. You recall from the last lecture that the key for Tocqueville was an accessible environment—that's what he meant by equality. The more accessible through equality, the lower the level of stimulation. Democratic societies fear stimulation, especially the stimulations of difference. And the more accessible an environment becomes to everyone, the lower the threshold of stimulation. It might seem that Simmel agrees. But, like any deep thinker, he was always arguing with himself. I'd like to read you just a passage, which I'll now cut from three pages to one paragraph, from an essay of Simmel's called "On the Tragedy and Conflict of Culture."

> Man often finds himself at the point of inter-
> section of two circles of objective forces
> and values. Each of which would like to drag
> him along. Often he feels himself to be the
> center who orders all life contents around him
> harmonically, according to the logic of his
> personality. And thus he feels solidarity with
> each of these circles, insofar as each belongs
> to a different circle and is claimed by another
> law of motion, his own.

And then he says:

> Thus our own essence forms an intersecting
> point of itself, with an alien circle of postulates.
> The process of culture, however, compresses
> the parties of this collision into extreme close
> contact by making the development of the
> subject conditional on the assimilation of the
> objective material.

And what that means is rather simple. When the conditions for
social conflict are destroyed in the city, individuals disappear.
That is, if the material basis of an urban civilization is destroyed,
if for instance you create a Co-op city, the will to assert an individuality loses its reason for being. And that's why the planning
of the material conditions of, on the one hand, overstimulation—
not just stimulation, but overstimulation, to take Hood's phrase,
"congestion is good"—and on the other hand, places where the
individual can withdraw from that stimulation, becomes essential
for the development of individuality.

Tocqueville thought that under a democratic tyranny there was no place to hide. Simmel thinks there is. He believes that the city casts a kind of protective veil of anonymity over the dissident. The repression possible in a small town isn't possible in a city. The greatest school of American urbanists at the University of Chicago in the 1920s took up this idea about the city as a protector of freedom. Because its very density and the tensions in it meant that no single group could ever dominate, which meant that people were free. If you take away anonymity in the city you take away people's freedom. Directly influenced by Simmel, this is how the Chicago School defined the relationship between urban form and freedom—and we still do. So, this is then how Simmel differs from Tocqueville: For Simmel, the city, by its very capacity to provide anonymity, puts a brake on democratic tyranny. What we are presented with here is a social psychology of a very static sort. There are these social conditions in the city that create the impetus for a person to assert himself or herself personally, but the creation of that individual won't transform the nature of the differences themselves—say by altering traffic patterns in a street. It's not a loop process. What he's interested in is how you arrive at the point in which a human being has a character that can be called distinctly urban, not what the social and political consequences are which form that character. And it's at that point where I, as it were, get off the bus with Simmel, because I think that urbanism can create that feedback loop. How to alter the quality of stimulation is the subject of the next lecture.

TWO KINDS OF COMMUNITY, NEITHER A SOLUTION

RICHARD: We've arrived at the midpoint in these lectures. And it's a rather disturbing point. Our goal is to try and understand in what ways city culture might become more democratic, and more broadly what it means to speak of the relationship between urban form and culture to democracy. You know that for a Greek this would be both a very puzzling and trivial question. It would be trivial because, for an Athenian in particular, democracy and urban culture were the same things. Even the word *polis* stands for both *political* and for *city*. They had just the one word. I think in the course of the first half of these lectures it's clear to us that that identity between urbanism, urban culture, and democracy is not something that we could in any way take for granted. We started in the first lectures, as you remember, by looking at the ways in which the foundation of democratic activity, which is discourse with people who are different, and what I call discourse with the other, was impeded or repressed in the development of modern cities in the name creating a kind of dominant political order.

In the second lecture, we looked at the way in which the desire for that discourse in modern democratic culture—democratic in the sense of Tocqueville—was weak. And in the last lecture we arrived at probably the most disturbing point of all in looking at this relationship. That is, we looked at some theories about the culture of modern cities, theories derived from the beginnings of modern urban thought, particularly with Simmel and Weber, which suggest that the kind of values of urban culture as a civilization—that is, what is valuable about city life—lead people to development of personality which at a certain point devalues the importance of discourse with them. There is an opposition between the kind of freedom in cities that makes people tolerant of those who are different and the importance attached to discourse. It's in this way from these three axes— from the vantage point of the imposition of silence, which has gone on as a tool of creating political order in modern cities, from the vantage point of mass desire, and most disturbingly of all, from the vantage point of what's good about the fragmentation of modern city culture, the kinds of freedom it creates— where a real tension in cross-purposes between urbanism and the democratic process seems to arise. Today I want to make this problem that appeared in the last lecture somewhat more concrete, and, as inevitably happens when you make something concrete, it gets to be more complex.

What does the specific issue of the existence of a community within the city as a whole mean for our overall problem? To answer that question, I'll have to solve a minor and trivial problem: What is a community? I'll somewhat cop out of an overall solution by talking about a particular kind of community life in cities, in which people have made a group identity for themselves in this city—that is, in which they haven't just entered into, and brought with them what we call in the sociological trade a set of ascribed characteristics of community, but make these characteristics appear. So, the kinds of urban communities I'm going to talk about are rather special, formed by people as not a passive matter of ascription but a conscious and volitional act. There are two distinct historical and social phases in which such voluntary communities emerge.

The first phase concerns the way the mass of foreign immigrants to American cities from 1880 to 1920 made themselves into communities in the city; the second kind of community I want to talk about is, and I use this word knowingly, is *us*— people like us, who react against the conditions of mass society in America. In the first case I'm talking about a very large phenomenon, statistically and historically, and I'm going to focus on only one aspect of it. In the second I'm talking about something that is, in terms of population, statistically insignificant, but I think revelatory in terms of understanding the relationship between urban culture and democracy. That is, how can people who are part of what Lionel Trilling once called the *adversary culture in America* use the conditions of city life to make communities for ourselves.

As always, I'd like to start with concrete human beings. The communities made en mass by immigrants are exemplified in this New York study I've alluded to in these lectures. Here I'll present to you three elderly immigrants who live in the West Village: they reflect about their lives when they first came to America. The first is from a retired Greek stevedore living in a boarding house. I've transformed all of this into standard English, which as you'll see when I come to the third is a problem. The Greek stevedore said to me:

> When I came here it was very strange.
> Strange to me that my food, my saints, all
> sorts of things mattered so much. People
> making a big deal about them. Many in my
> line of work sees a lot of different types,
> different people, but I'm trying to say, you
> know, for instance, that the Greek loves
> to dance, the Greek man dances. Well, in
> Piraeus we would just dance.

Piraeus is the port for Athens.

> We would dance. And the men off the boats
> from other places would watch and we would
> teach them. Here in New York, everybody
> told me, "Don't dance, don't let them see you
> dancing, they will think it strange and that
> you aren't a good American."

Next door to this stevedore lived an elderly but still very active Italian doctor, a remarkably intelligent man, who came to America from Palermo: I described to him his Greek neighbor's statement—I should say that this is a technique of interviewing called *response interviewing*. It takes a group of people and confronts one with the responses of another, and confronts a third with the responses of the two before. Rather than assuming the informant is a kind of tabula rasa who just speaks and gives you data, it creates a community of reaction to what other people have said. Then you bring them all together. It's a way of trying to specify how to concretely see others. The way people react to each other in a community. —————— The Italian doctor reacted to the Greek stevedore as follows:

> Yes, quite true. Americans made so much of
> these differences. The American way of life,
> we were always being told we had to become
> part of it, to cover up our past. When I first
> came here, I had, thanks to a refugee agency—

He came in 1936.

> —a place in a clinic in a small town in
> Oklahoma. The people were desperately poor,
> almost as poor as in Sicily, but they didn't
> want me to treat them. They didn't trust me
> because I was dark-skinned. By luck I had
> distant relatives here and so could come to
> New York. I became, how shall I say, more
> Italian in America than in Sicily. I was made
> so much more aware of it. The ones older than
> me, poor uneducated men, even more so.
> They thought in the old country of belonging
> to a village. The man who lived fifty kilome-
> ters away was a foreigner. You see, there was
> in the old country there a clear inside–outside,
> belonging–not belonging. Here no one felt
> comfortable with the Americans and they
> were so disdainful of us, so we had to remake
> everything. A new category called Italian.
> Calabrese, Piedmontese, Siciliana, all together,
> all not belonging. That was the life of the
> Italians in New York.

Across the street lived in elderly Polish-Jewish accountant,
who reacted in turn to these views as follows:

> Our neighborhood is more like a potlatch than
> a borscht.

How can we make this clearer in Harvard—this bastion of
New England puritanism? A potlatch is a soup that has a little
of everything in it, I suppose, and a borscht is more pure.

It was taken badly when we moved here from
the Lower East Side.

That is, this is a man who deserted the Lower East Side to come
live in this community, which as I mentioned to you before was
the place where Jane Jacobs originally wrote and used as a sort
of model for *The Death and Life of Great American Cities*.

To desert your own kind. I know that doctor.
Very smart man, educated. Of course it was
true. Lots of people like you around. You
felt safer in the Lower East Side. In the course
for us it was worse, always worse for Jews.
So that others looked at it bad when I left the
Lower East Side. They said we've all got
to stay together. I didn't want the goyim—

That I shouldn't have to translate.

—but I didn't want that either. Poland was
bad for Jews when I was a boy. Why should I
become a Pole here?

You can see from these three interviews the aspect of immigration in the United States that I want to focus on—that people were made to have an identity here. They became Poles here, they became Italians here. Most of them came from very small villages, and the compass of social reality was confined to that village. They had a sense of being inside and being able to place people outside. When they came here, they were shocked into a new kind of consciousness of themselves, which was a collective category. ——— An older generation of urban historians tends to look at the process as one of uprooting and a kind of individual isolation, and a kind of total disorientation. Thanks to some more recent studies of urban migration, we know this view isn't quite so. For instance, there was a great deal of block migration, especially to second-order industrial communities—communities like Pittsburgh and Buffalo— where block migration meant a whole village would be moved, often through a labor contractor in the old country that would ship them all together. In other words, it was economic. You made more cash if you could deliver 150 bodies instead of one. It wasn't far from being a kind of market in bodies. And for some reason that kind of block negotiation went on with sort of second-order cities. There was also a lot more of what Virginia Yans in a recent book called *stream migration*—that is, the reconstituting of an old village or territory in American cities.

Two or three families come and they might send back the money to the parents, the nephews, and so on, and gradually you have a stream of reconstitution. In other words, what we've been finding out about urban migration is that it's much more collective in its means. Still, there was a jolt psychologically caused by this migration process. The jolt is beautifully described in Oscar Handlin's *The Uprooted*—the jolt into having an identity and being forced to have an identity in America, and then having to deal with how to take that ascription in as an element of oneself, from having an ascribed set of characteristics to absorbing these and making a community out of them. American cities and suburbs were built very rapidly and in large tracts. Investment under these conditions was made most profitable if all the houses were the same level. This is very much like our Haussmann problem. Entrepreneurs then mass-produced environments, and then later we had practices like redlining by banks, which reinforced this kind of homogeneity.

Conditions in the city led people to convert ethnic and racial stereotypes into the materials for a common collective community life. The first of them was made quite clear by both the Italian and the Jew in the interviews that I've cited is the sheer density of the turn-of-the-century cities. The larger the city, the more concentrated were people of an ethnicity, and there was a sense of strength in that: the shield of numbers, rather than being a lone or nearly lone foreigner. The first element of what cities did for this old pattern of identity formation was to create conditions of density that made people feel safe. The Italian felt it, and the Jew also felt it but it made him very uncomfortable. What's interesting about this interview was how other people treated him when he'd say, "No, I didn't want to be, I was a Jew in the old country, I didn't want to be a Pole, why should I be a Pole here in America."

The second thing about the first wave of community, unique to the physical building of American cities, was tenement construction. The only place these tenements permitted large numbers of people any sociability was outside on the streets. Think about the architecture of tenement construction in New York—long, long railroad flats extending back to eighty-six feet? I'm sure somebody tomorrow will tell me I'm wrong. In any event, very, very long with the inner air shafts facing blank walls. The only place to have any contact with other people was outside the building. There was more street life in communities that had these tenement constructions than in two- or three-family houses in the outskirts of Brooklyn or the beginnings of Queens in the nineteenth century. The very inhumanity of the tenements forced people out on the streets, and this created the conditions for a kind of street economy, with peddlers selling in the streets.

Jacob Riis, Mulberry Bend, c. 1896.

Moreover, there was an economic hole in the investment pattern of cities at the end of the nineteenth century. The dominant forms of investment were capital intensive in large-scale industries. What this meant is that the service sector opened up; it was empty economic space colonized in the ghettos by immigrant labor. I mean, J. P. Morgan was not interested in dry cleaning. The one exception to that of course is the garment district and the garment industry in New York. Since the profitable returns on capital were in large forms of industrial enterprise in big cities, the absence in the economy immigrants filled was more family labor than individual enterprise, starting with the buying of small stores. The familiar story—the family that struggles and finally buys a deli or a dry-cleaning plant—has shifted now; ghetto-dwellers cannot repeat the Hispanic or native Black story that began in the 1910s and 1920s. The service industry is now a very profitable form of investment for dominant financial institutions. This is a fact always conveniently forgotten by people who say, "We did it, why can't they?"

Lastly, this kind of community took hold as a community because the immigrants could actually stimulate house-building. There was a looseness in the boundaries of American cities. A city like New York was like an accordion from 1880 to 1920, and the notion of protecting a territory didn't exist. The same thing was true to an even greater degree in Chicago. Like natives living on the land, they were continually moving. So, then, what you had was a kind of lung that allowed these people to accrete and to build communities for themselves, or, for the people who would put them in tenements, to build tenements that they then would then rent to locals. That's a very different pattern than, for instance, what happened in Paris after the Algerian war, when you had large numbers of *peids-noir* coming into the city. There was tremendous competition for territory—competition between Turks, *peids-noir*, and Spanish immigrant labor around Paris. The result was a dispersal pattern, where you had little blocks of *peids-noir* all around Paris and little blocks of Turks all around Paris, and you never had these massive agglomerations of people together.

Forced to turn inward upon themselves, they obviously had no dialog with the Other. Apart from halting English, the natives didn't want to speak to them because they were foreign. I'm trying to make a very simple point. These people were people for whom the creation of community had no implication of democracy in the sense we're talking about. The community comes from an assigned identity. People had to convert that ascription into a shared life. I make this point in order to contrast it to the created sense of identity in places like the West Village. As I said, it is statistically small but it's culturally significant. Here people want to resist the sorts of conformity pressures that Tocqueville described, such as we explored in the second lecture. I want to make clear that I'm talking about *us*, we who have been called the *adversarial culture* or the *cultural edge*, we try to use the city to create a life against the mass. The question I want to pose is this: How can such an adversarial identity become democratic?

Let me illustrate that possibility by returning to the West Village. Its elderly migrants lived from the 1940s to the late 1960s in an ethnically and racially mixed community, also with artists and stevedores. In the early 1970s, as I told you, before the community began to change and become gentrified, the middle class who were moving in were mostly single, young, and middle-aged men. I think it's the largest concentration of gay people in the city. Today there are about 15,000 single men between the ages of twenty-one and thirty-nine living in an area that's bounded by Seventh Avenue, 14th Street, the West Side Highway, and Vandam Street, I think, is the bottom of that census area. That's about twenty square blocks. It's a huge concentration of single, middle-class, youngish middle-aged men. Few of the people in this new population were born in New York City let alone in Greenwich Village. There are migrants from small towns from the interior who come to New York because for the first time they can live and work without repressive restrictions. They disrupted the past and have come to mark themselves in public as having an identity. It's now a very familiar iconography of sexual preference, wherein one wears a handkerchief to indicate one's particular sexual desires and so on. They've also driven out the Mafia from the neighborhood and from most of the shops. In New York one of the things the Mafia did was to try and control all the gay bars and businesses. By being an external control, there were all sorts of things that went on—I mean, sometimes the Mafia would arrange raids to clean out a particular bar, and the extortion that went on. It was not a happy business. They converted sexual preference into a crime, and they made a lot of money out of it. But they've been driven out, and several of their shops and restaurants are now owned by gay men and patronized by gay men.

An identity, psychologist Erik Erikson wrote, is a negotiation between intrapsychic life and external social reality. It's a negotiation that he believes a human being conducts at the end of adolescence and the onset of adulthood. I'm not going to say very much about the intrapsychic side of the matter, but I want to talk about the social side of the matter, particularly the way in which America forces its citizens who react against mass society to keep continually renegotiating their identities throughout their lives. If I can extend Erikson's analogy to diplomacy for a moment: each treaty of personal, willful, voluntary identity an urbanite tries to sign challenges conditions beyond his control. It's a paradox. An internal exile from an ascribed community requires living in a city; impersonal, disturbing, dislocating—not a local, cohesive community. That's the point that I want to make at the end of this lecture.

The need to be conscious of the Other appears in an autobiographic fragment by James Q. Wilson. He writes of his childhood in Southern California in the 1940s as follows:

> People had no identities except their personal identities, no obvious group affiliations to make possible any reference to them by collective nouns. I never heard the phrase "ethnic group" until I was in graduate school. I never knew there were Irishmen (I was amazed many years later to learn that, at least on my mother's side, I had been one all along) or Italians (except funny organ grinders in the movies, all of whom looked like Chico Marx). We knew there were Negroes (but none within miles of where we lived) and Jews (they ran Hollywood and New York, we knew, but not many of us had ever met one). Nobody ever even pointed out to me that I was a Catholic (except once, when a friend explained that was probably the reason I wouldn't join the order of DeMolay, a young people's Masonic group).

In order to become a more distinct person, Wilson had to acquire an awareness of others—others who he could not become. He had to learn to become, if I may put it this way, one among many.

Before, Wilson tells us, he knew there were Jews and Black people but their presence never impinged on his life, nor did the fact of their existence have any reality. Without difference, there is no presence, no sense of who he is. You understand here that this fragment—indeed the whole memoir, which is a marvelous piece of work—connects to the Tocquevillian theme that the way in which you create equality is by eradicating a consciousness of difference. Wilson felt that this lack of awareness meant that therefore his own life was a blank. If there's no difference, then there's no presence and no sense of who he is. But the awareness of the Other is of an unbridgeable gap.

I hope this fragment from Wilson's memoir makes clear that society makes acquiring an identity a struggle when it veils the reality of human differences. "Society" in this Tocquevillian, mass sense. Society can also make the struggle unfair because the recovery occurs when it's too late, when one's place has already been defined. This theme is similar in the memoirs of Americans from very different backgrounds. Recovery of a social self and discovery of difference are set against a neutralizing social order. In the *Autobiography of Malcolm X*, the young man discovers what it means to be Black in America. The child kept in isolation knew nothing of racism. He had to learn he was Black. America for Malcolm X, as for James Q. Wilson, casts a veil over difference in childhood. And in popular fiction, like Ellen Schwamm's recent novel *Adjacent Lives*, women are presented as coming to consciousness of themselves as women only after the first throws of the dice have been made in their lives—marriage, children, an affair—and then afterward the consciousness of who one was when one was acting. Society appears not as a clearly built prison, but in Schwamm's words "as a fog." Now, some of the social controls we've explored earlier in this lecture, and in the other lectures in the series, explained these feelings of being identity-less, of being in a fog.

When the writer James T. Farrell says, "It took me in the midst of the Great Depression until the age of thirty to know that I was working class," he's not expressing a purely personal blindness. You know this refers to a very longstanding problem in this country of a kind of refusal of class consciousness. He is expressing how, in the midst of the most severe economic degradation, the social order of segregation can work to make an American feel blank. The little molecule becomes the universal measure of life. Outside becomes alien, hostile, and it's hard to think of penetrating it. The outside is obscured. Of course from American cities from the end of the nineteenth century onward to create ghettos for Black people, ethnic groups, and social classes, the political consequence is a loss of consciousness. If you're not Black, or Italian, you won't see them. Like Wilson in Los Angeles, you are blissfully naive. It's been true in America, as it was after the Civil War, as it was true in bourgeois France, that what Robert Wiebe has called the *search for order* involved the notion of the separation of potentially hostile social groups. So, again, there's been a political attempt to keep these groups apart. Wiebe points to political machines like Tammany Hall in New York as not the great instrument of integration in American life as it's sometimes thought, as by Richard Wade, but essentially as means to enforce segregation— that is, the political machine was a way for each group to solve its own problems internally, distributing a kind of largesse that came from the top to the leaders of the machine, but at the price of ordinary citizens having rights and standing in the city.

The assertion of one's apartness, one's place in a society as one among many is politically significant for two reasons. It's post-factum, after the fact, forming a sense of difference-ness and related-ness after you've been initially formed by the environment. It's made against the "fog" of society, rebelling against the phenomenon of neutralization in the dominant culture. I really want you to understand this, because these are political consequences of making an identity. In a book like Jean-Paul Sartre's *Les Mots*—*The Words*—which is his autobiography, you would find something that for us as Americans is really quite incomprehensible. The young Sartre, the boy of eight or ten, knows the social map. He knows the contours of the bourgeois world, the working-class world, and the elite world. Society is transparent. Those class distinctions are made clear. Sartre is therefore constantly afraid of violating himself by participating in a society whose compromises, lies, and demands he understands only too well. Whereas Malcolm X thought himself nowhere, which is an entirely different form of political self-harm. Sartre could deceive himself and ruin his authenticity by doing what he knows would be bourgeois. For Malcolm X the problem was that he didn't know how a Black person should behave as a Black person. That was his problem of identity, and that was something he therefore had to create.

The Tocquevillian question is, how does one emerge from being nowhere? The social side of the answer lies in creating what Lionel Trilling calls an adversary culture. Not simply develop a set of personality characteristics but create a community of resistance; not just saying I'm a particular creature. Accepting that there are others in the same position as yourself, and unlike yourself. Those who feel themselves in what Trilling called the adversary culture are in search of this special sort of community. The city as we now know it can create such a community, set against the mores of mass life. ———— That is, I think, for people like us, what we're talking about when we talk about community. We're not talking about a consumption society. We're not talking about more supermarkets, or the instant access of vacuum cleaner stores and the like just around the corner. What people in an adversary culture want is richer than all that. Of course, "we" aren't so ordinary, are we?

You remember we talked about Walter Benjamin and Georg Simmel in this connection. These analyses of stimulus and shock bear on a pronounced American social value. It involves thirst for "real" experiences. The real experiences that count in forming an identity have to be acquired. The language of possession is used by Americans, or, more primitively and more accurately, an analogy to eating is used. Americans speak of being hungry for real experiences and of wanting, in Henry James's phrase, to "gorge themselves on real life." Simply to live, to go shopping, to go out to the office, to take care of the children, to experience the waning of life, to chat with the neighbors, this is not real life and is not real experience. Nor does transitory sensation count in itself as a real experience. A disruption must occur. By disrupting the routines of living, you know who you are and where you are, which is the American translation of that notion of culture formed by shock that we talked about last time in Simmel and made references to in the work of Benjamin.

Let me give a much less highfalutin example of this, drawn from the interviews in my New York study, this time with a group of working-class Catholic women. These women had begun to use birth control devices in defiance of the Church about six years ago, and at the time I was interviewing them, again with this technique of interviewing that I described to you, one of them had had an abortion that all knew about and discussed. They were all stably married. They were committing a sin according to the Church, but they did not view themselves as directly confronting religious authority. Rather, these disruptions of routine signified to them for the first time that they had particularized their desires. By using birth control devices, they became special people in the Catholic community. They expressed the sense of particularizing their desire in terms of the vividness of the experiences they were having. For instance, somebody said, "Now I really feel sex. I don't worry about where to get money to feed the next baby when I make love." It's a kind of typical comment. The notion of having acquired some reality in one's life as a matter of something that belongs to you as an individual was a matter of disruption, not of social isolation. It seems a great contrast to Tocqueville's use of the word *individual*.

The urban element, for these people, appeared for me in doing these interviews when I asked them about the social controls exercised on the Church by them. What was clear was that in the city the fragmentation of the power of any one institution like the Church, but even more importantly the multiplicity of contacts they had, that is to say—they all went to church, by the way, and of course would never confess to the priest because he just wouldn't understand, but they all thought of themselves as devout Catholics—there were so many other ways of thinking about themselves as related to life in the city, so many other kinds of identifications they make—like with work, with the local machine, some of them were with the Mafia, and so on— that the notion of being under the moral suasion of one organic moral order didn't exist for them.

This goes back to the point we've been talking about through-out these lectures: in the terms in which modern urban culture exists, freedom comes from a fragmenting of a single, dominant set of controls. But for these particular women that fragmen-tation meant they had lots of different connections and lots of different particular realities to test what they were doing. That's the kind of intervention in identity formation that the city can produce. Even more than fragmentation is the possibility of making what Louis Wirth, one of the Chicago School urbanists, once called a *multiplicity of identifications*, something that finally allows a person to disrupt routine in any one of them. Is that clear? That you can only disrupt a routine when you don't feel you're pulling down the whole world. The more multiple your sense of the realities you live in, the more flexible does the possibility of shaking any one of them become. The city can give you the sense of being connected in a lot of ways. For these women the result is, as appeared in our interviews, that they're much more sensitive to those other people than women who have not at all challenged the church. Having disrupted the norm, and having made a sense of themselves as different, has also made them much more aware of those who were afraid to have abortions.

If I could summarize it, I would say that the organization of identity in city life comes from exiting normality in society as a whole. American literature is suffused with this imagery of the city as an instrument for shocking people out of their insensibility, and in the process furnishing them with the emotional material to form counteridentities for themselves. Novels that are as different in time and social milieux as Theodore Dreiser's *Sister Carrie* and Hubert Selby's portraits of contemporary New York show it. It's also why there's this tremendous love-hate relationship. The kind of thing Morton and Lucia White talk about in their book *The Intellectual Versus the City: From Thomas Jefferson to Frank Lloyd Wright,* about cities in our country. Urban liberation may not seem so different in other countries. The American version is that you're forced into having the burden of setting yourself against a neutral mass.

In our country, it might seem to speak well for the dominant institutions, since they're not so powerful after all. This conclusion would be an error. The complexity of domination in American society is that the dominant institutions can permit people to form voluntary communities of identity and then use them, robbing the effort of any real value. The sting of difference is solved by toleration. Toleration is a peculiar mirror of equality. The mirror is different from the mirror of Tocqueville's mass Americans, as represented in his first volume of *Democracy in America*. There is no attempt to force everyone to have the same identity, which indeed would destroy the meaning of the search for identity itself, nor is there a mirror of equality in the sense Tocqueville imagined in the second volume of *Democracy*. He imagined individualism as a private matter, something kept secret from the public realm. He imagined the public realm as listless and empty. The conundrum of identity in modern America—the identity created for us, those in the adversary culture—is the distinctive identities people find for themselves and attempt to share with each other to structure something in common. It is precisely the bringing of identity into the public realm—making it communal—that creates a public. For once out in public, collective identities based on racial solidarity, sexual freedom, and ethnic revival are likely to be absorbed, trivialized, and neutralized by the dominant culture.

At this point, I want to reference a remarkable book called *Ethnic Chauvinism: The Reactionary Impulse* by a sociologist who teaches at Harvard, Orlando Patterson. It made much of what's I've argued clear to me. In the way of many good books, it has suffered from neglect. I think it's out of print. Patterson argues that self-conscious attempts to assert ethnic identity set against the dominant institutions can be self-defeating. That happens where identities are put on parade—presented as static, fixed. They confront but do not interact with power. The parade does not invite discussion. They're an expression of helplessness in speaking the language of power, parading as a kind of defiant cultural strength.

A controversy has arisen in the gay rights movement about whether communities like the West Village represent the achievement of freedom or a parade of identity, an empty badge of identity. Dennis Altman, for instance, has argued that a self-created ghetto has replaced the pressure to keep one's life a secret. His opponents argue that freedom lies in confronting others with whom one really is—the parade is political, the theatre matters even if there is no dialog with the audience. In slang there's an argument about clones—about people who dress and groom to make themselves as visible as possible to others in public. Is a clone instantly recognizable as gay, a political icon, a person breaking out of the American fog? That is, this community I'm studying is an instance of people who really have created a community that is a rebellion made out of the phenomenon of community, a rebellion against being absolutely neutral, being forced to be neutral in the mass society. Patterson's argument is, "No." American Black and Hispanic people have fallen into a trap, the trap of parading one's identity and using the streets as a vehicle for publication. Cities both stimulate people to publish their identities and make it safe and possible for them to do so. "You do your thing. I do mine."

I'd like to consider what this tolerant formation of community of identity means in a philosophical sense. Michel Foucault and I argued in a recent essay, which is in the *London Review of Books* from June 3, 1981, that the only viable concept of freedom in the modern state is an existence that escapes definition and categorization. The reason is that all the agencies of power in modern society are bent upon enlarging their controls and manipulating those through whom they control through an ever-greater knowledge of them, in what we call in our article the *net of classification*. Self-identification is a way of weaving that net for the powerful. For example, identities literally become consumption items over time degraded into fashion. Today this occurs for instance in the mass consumption of ghetto Black fashion, which has become chic. In the degradation of identity struggles into titillating tastes to be mass consumed—consumed first with a sense of daring and later with a more numb sense that the emblems of someone else's identity make one interesting—desire itself is neutralized. The deeper attitudes are subject to the same process: the more they are iconic, the less defiant they become.

It's in this way, we argue, that the production of identities ultimately feeds the dominant culture. In the second volume of *Democracy in America*, Tocqueville depicted private desire and public life as two separate realms. A century and a half later, traffic has been established between these two realms. A rebellious private is gradually being neutralized and weakened in public. Rebellions against the blandness of the public realm gradually pass over into the public realm itself, consumed there. Such absorption relates more to Tocqueville than to Marx. The market does not create divisions in society as Marx thought, rather it neutralizes division and it trivializes the admirable desire to have an identity, to have a sense of who you are, who you are not, and who is different—the market trivializes this impulse by making it in the end safely.——— Now, if this were the whole matter we might conclude as follows: Tocqueville has just said all that needs to be explained. Everyone in public is in fact rendered similar. The market has simply had the effect of exhausting private passion. But our society is not so static. Precisely the using up of identities creates the sense of emptiness that sets people in motion looking for new ones. An American can pass through many identities in a lifetime, and each tells him he is someone special who inhabits a demarcated space. As the badges of self are trivialized, he looks for new ones, and this is what creates the tremendous instability of American community life of this sort, why these communities are so terribly short-lived.

Still, it's in voluntary communities where people invested passion. This is a personal aside, but I'm thinking of the commune where I lived at Putnam Avenue and Western Avenue in Cambridge in the 1960s. It was a place people put years and years of their lives into, and then all at once it just vanished. And this is more largely true of adversarial communities in America. I don't think our experience was much different from those elsewhere. There's a tremendous initial energy in the investment, so that the sudden demise of these communities may seem puzzling. But once people wear a badge of identity others can recognize, the place becomes fatally vulnerable to tolerant absorption. Which is more complicated than it might appear. Without a badge or gay clothes or Afro speech or ethnic Catholicism, how can you relate your newly found self to the lives of other people? ——— No human being can or should have the burden of establishing within one lifetime a complete sense of world, but that, in a certain sense, is the peculiar problem of urban culture. We are forced to make this effort because of routine, fixity, and tradition in our lives. For us the ordinary is, again in Henry James's phrase, a slum. The poverty of experience is usually signified by those endless rows of California houses that James Q. Wilson describes. It's a truly demanding task to leave this experiential slum. So I've come to think of identity in the formation of voluntary communities of identity in cities as a kind of work of Sisyphus, in response to the habits of everyday life.

To conclude, I'm afraid all this is a long and tortuous explanation for what I believe to be the starting point for any meaningful democratic politics in the city, to which I turn next. In the last two lectures we will explore how the communal, social, and even architectural structure of cities can be planned so that a transcendence of identity can occur in the public realm. ——— Thank you.

THE TOWN SQUARE

RICHARD: I don't know if you know the phrase of Santayana called *tissues of difference*—it's an idea he developed in an essay about the notion that a human culture takes form only by attachments between people who are different. These tissues grow in town squares. Town squares aren't very strong in modern society, and certainly not in modern cities. So, what I'm going to describe is more prospective than descriptive. I haven't spoken much about the visual aspects of cities up to this point, because I wanted to prepare the social and political grounds, as it were, but I think we're ready to consider how urban form intersects with urban democracy in the town square. We're going to consider this visual social intersection in a concrete way—how forms are imagined by a group I'm going to call the new urbanists.

By the new urbanists I mean to identify and reclassify some architects and architectural theorists who otherwise have been called postmodernists, specifically Manfredo Tafuri, Aldo Rossi, the Krier brothers, Colin Rowe, Fred Koetter, and Ricardo Bofill. I'm going to assume some knowledge of their work on your part. If you lack it, let me recommend an easy introduction: a book by Charles Jencks called *The Language of Post-Modern Architecture.* Another is an excellent article by Dan Graham in the current December 1981 *Artforum* called, and here's the whole title, "Not Post-Modernism: History as Against Historicism, European Archetypal Vernacular in Relation to the American Commercial Vernacular, and the City as Opposed to the Individual Building." Much of what I have to say fits in with Graham's article. I also recommend it to you because a particular building project of Rossi's that I'm going to discuss is very well illustrated in the article.

I want to discuss these designers as new urbanists rather than postmodernists, because that latter label suggests they are simply in the state of reaction modernism and its visual vocabulary, when in fact they have shifted the focus of design in the last decade from building *in* an environment to building *an* environment. They've attempted to rethink the position of the designer from that of a man or a woman living in this environment, the place becoming beyond the designer's control and acquiring a form beyond the designer's stamp. The term *postmodern* in design has, as such sweeping classifications always do, linked too many disparate figures together. As you know, people like Robert Venturi have been linked with the people I've just mentioned, whereas his recourse to history and his sense of the vernacular is much different and much more shallow than, say, the ideas and plans of Rossi, who has elaborated a theory of collective memory to guide his sense of visual imagery. In the same way there's as much difference to be found among these new urbanists as there is similarity.

I mention them because I want to describe the requisites for a community of difference. First of all, is it a place? I think it is. I think it is a concrete place: a square, a center. This is an architecture that has a geography. This group of new urbanists has been trying to build "tissues of difference," but without the theoretical self-understanding of what they were doing; often the designs went wrong, so that the results of their efforts defeated the purpose of creating an environment both complex and free. ——— In the first part of this lecture I want to define more fully the idea of a town square as being a community of difference. In the second part, in discussing these urbanists, I want to chart the various attempts in the last decade to envision this town square as a place. Here is a paradoxical, not to say unfair critique. I'll discuss whether a project meets criteria the architect never had in mind, and which I only had in mind six months ago. I'm going to ask how and in what way we can see the requisites and instruments of the community of difference, and what happens when the attempt to see them goes wrong. In the third part of the lecture—and there's so much to this that I'll probably skim over it very lightly—I want to assay, if you or I could learn to build this ideal town square, would people ever want to live in it? To begin, I want to describe this prospective community of difference in terms of two modes. In one mode abstract requisites rule, and in the second concrete requirements shape the ideal town square.

There are eight abstract requisites for such a place. The first responds to the problems of identity that we discussed in the last lecture. In that lecture, we talked about the ways in which urban communities, which are consciously made as projecting a common collective identity, are remarkably fragile in modern capitalist society—remarkably fragile and often very fratricidal. They're more fragile than the kind of ethnic communities in which an identity is assigned in cities—as in the immigrant communities we also discussed in the last lecture. Still, an ideal community of difference can support people to live beyond the terms of ascription. Let me give you an example of what I mean by that. In New York there's an attempt to distribute funds from the city by using the census to take a very detailed account of people's origins, whether they're Black or white, whether they were born in Puerto Rico or the Dominican Republic, and so on. The idea is that by assessing places of origin means the city is likely to be disadvantaged. This seems to me to be absolutely the wrong way to create a town square. Rather than recognizing participation in it, it narrows support in the community to a statistic about a label—the very essence of ascription.

The second requisite rule is that there must be enough points of multiple contact so that single versions of identity can be shifted or transcended. For instance, if you have a community—to take an example we used in the last lecture—of 15,000 gay men and very few other people as in the far West Village—or if you have a community of 15,000 to 20,000 Mormons who have all chosen to go to the same place, this can never become a truly civic space, a place where differences meet. Multiplicity of contact makes it possible to think of yourself in that community as not being limited to one kind of identity. Jane Jacobs didn't believe it was possible to have intermixture without integration, which seems to me to miss the point. To me, you get a town square when somebody is able to have physical contact with someone else who's different, yet able to keep a sense of being separate persons. This is the ideal of living one among many. This ideal translates in space through compressing many people physically in contact.

So, the first of these two abstract requisite rules for a community of difference is that people are able to live beyond the statistic terms of their assigned identity, and that there are enough physical points of multiple contact, enough compression in the community to sensitize people to the presence of others. The next three—I'm sorry, I really want to do this in a systematic way, this is a theory, and I know it's boring to listen to a theory, but thinking doesn't always let us have a good time—the next three of these requisite rules for community have to do with the problem of democratic domination that we looked at in the second lecture. Tocqueville's analysis of mass society involved issues more subtle than conformism. Still, he recognized that majority rule tends to universalize its decisions, as though all should believe what the majority decides. In order to deal with that problem, the following three requisite rules seem to have to be met in an ideal town square. First is embodied in the American Bill of Rights: that there are rights which transcend democratic process. A polity cannot vote to expel minorities. The will of a majority cannot be universalized.

The fourth requisite rule would be that the political organization of discussion and debate about communal problems is not limited to occasions when decisions must be made. Tocqueville again critiqued the mechanization of democracy. He talked about the ways in which to pressure in a democratic society is to routinize the notion of democratic discourse so that it's always concerned with making a decision. There is no such thing as discourse that doesn't have as its object the production of a decision. That, for Tocqueville, was tyrannical, because a decision means that ultimately you have to simplify things to *yes or no*, or *choose one of the four*. In the ideal town square, discussion is continuous. I think this is intuitively obvious. You discuss things much better, more fully, when you're not under the pressure to make a decision about them. That is to say, you learn more in informal situations like chatting in a bar than formal debates and point-scoring in a voting chamber. People drink and smoke in our ideal town square.

Derived from that is the fifth and my most draconian requisite rule for such a place: that an individual loses legitimate standing by failing to participate in these non-decision-making occasions, but loses no legitimacy by failing to participate in the decision-making. You must go to the cafe. I've been told this is quite dreadful. I want to explain what I mean. We recall from Tocqueville that one of the pressures in a community was the notion of surrender, of discourse for the sake of being left alone in a private realm. Tocqueville envisioned a kind of contrary pressure: that of encouraging people to participate in voluntary organizations in order to be taken seriously. What I envision is an expansion of such a non-instrumental association in order to be respected. A person who does not belong to unions, who eschews appearing in public places, who keeps to himself or herself, has no legitimacy in the ideal town square. ———
In the very first lecture on power and silence, we saw there was—characteristic of a modern city—an attempt to create order through modes of social and economic segregation. The last three requisite rules deal with that. The sixth of our eight, and the first of these three, is that the town square has to be boundaryless. Every center should be open to the outside.

The seventh of these rules, derived from the sixth, is that the community has a right to resist parts from whole planning. The great dilemma of large-scale planning is what I called in my book *The Uses of Disorder*—referring to the 1930s and 1940s in this country and Great Britain—the derivative principle. The idea being that one establishes a set of goals for a city as a whole, or for a regional plan as a whole, and then one derives how they should be applied to the parts of the city. What that does is absolutely devalue any expression of the reaction to it by the people who live in that community. You have a kind of higher principle, which is a principle of derivation. What those large-scale plans did, and the kinds of things city-planning associations were doing, was assert that it is more legitimate to derive the life of the parts from the existence of a whole plan than it is to take seriously the discourse that people in those parts would have with each other. A community always has the right to resist impositions from the outside, based on an ideology of parts from whole. ———— The eighth and final of these abstract requisite rules is that a conflict between communities can only be resolved through negotiation. Again, it's illegitimate to use master plans or regional plans as a rationale to impose form on a community without negotiation.

Let me summarize all of these requisite rules. You can't have a town unless the following eight conditions are met. First, it's a community in which persons can live beyond the terms of prescribed identity—they are not pinioned, as we do in New York, through distribution by way of censuses of origins. Second, there are enough physical points of multiple contact so that the person's experience lets them transcend the identities they've been assigned. Third, there is no universalization of decision-making—for example, a community can't vote to expel minorities. Fourth, political organization of discussion and debate about communal problems is not limited to occasions when decisions must be made. Fifth, an individual loses standing and respect by failing to participate in these non-decision-making occasions for debate, but loses no rights by failing to participate in decision making. Sixth, the community is open to the outside, and can be boundaryless if it so desires. Seventh, the community has a right to resist part-from-whole planning. And eighth, conflict between communities can only be resolved through negotiation—that it's illegitimate to impose master plans or regional plans on the community without negotiation. If you don't follow these rules—if these conditions aren't met—the town square can't exist. And, conversely, to make it exist, these ways power works need to be realigned.

I told you that these ideas are utopian. ———— Turning now to the concrete requirements that would need to be met for such a gathering space, they involve two major issues: first, the generation of diversity, and second, the generation of sociability. In the 1960s urban theorists and urban designers had a fairly good idea of the spatial forms of diversity. There are three of them: numbers, density, and functional intermixture. People like Lynn Loflin, for instance, in a book called *A World of Strangers* shows that each of these generates diversity on distinctly urban terms. If you have 10,000 people in one place, for example, the interaction between them will produce more diverse forms of communication and belief than if those same 10,000 people were organized in units of 100 and the degree of interaction was limited to 100 groups of 100 people. This is something that Loflin has taken great pains to argue.

In his book *Crowding and Behavior*, Jonathan Freedman made the same point and the same argument about density—that if you have those 10,000 people and they're spread over a three-square-mile area, the degree to which you'll produce difference is less than if they're compacted into a one-mile area. I've made the same argument about functional intermixture. You are more likely to produce economic spinoffs in a diverse and concentrated space. I won't get into the technicalities of it, but if you had twenty diamond businesses in one area, you would be less likely to create external revenue for the community than you would if you had five diamond businesses, five delis, five seamstress shops, and five bookstores on the same block. The notion is wrong that a concentration of similarity produces a kind of capital base for cities that is greater than that produced by intermixtures of business. In sum, numbers, density, and functional intermixture each has a function in producing diversity—not in just agglomerating it, but in creating synergies.

For the generation of sociability in the town square, a rather different set of conditions must be met. I'd argue that the first of them is a clear articulation of the distinction between public and private. I took some of you around Jane Jacobs's West Village housing project in New York on Saturday, and if you compare that to, say, the Arab Quarter in Jerusalem, which some of us are only too well acquainted with by this time in the term, the difference in those two communities is that Jane Jacobs and the planners associated with her destroy an articulation between public and private space, whereas in the Arab community there is a very highly articulated difference between the two. Now, putting aside the cultural differences one wants to talk about, the reason the Jane Jacobs space feels dead and the Arab space seems to encourage people and put everything else aside to encourage a kind of public sociability, I would argue, is because you only get informal participation when a community draws a line between the personal and the social. Eight abstract requisite rules draw this line. This is the whole point of my book *The Fall of Public Man*: public space should be a protection against the private domain. I'm not going to explain this conundrum just now, but am just flatly asserting that in order to generate sociability there's got to be a clear articulation between public and private so that people feel free in public.

The second condition that needs to be met in order to produce sociability is that public structures have to be planned for overload rather than for coordination. This is based on Raymond Hood's famous statement that "congestion is good." I believe you can't have a town square unless there's an overload of input, in terms of the domain of sociability. Bars, restaurants, parks, and so on. There are a couple of reasons for this: one, the most obvious, is that it creates activity in the community. The second is that it prohibits exclusionary boundaries. We looked in the first lecture at the campusization effect of planning; planning provides no more than what an external power defines as its needs. That inevitably means that one external agency can provide it. If you say X community needs Y number of bars, or—something more practical—a community needs a supermarket of such and such size, it is easy for the same planner to find somebody to build it, and own it. To stimulate internal activity, you need to plan for an overload of inputs and outcomes, for too much possibly happening. People sensing this possibility will more likely get engaged than if they feel they are living in a well-oiled machine. Too much invites engagement; just enough invites passivity.

What visually underlies these two concrete requirements is a certain concept of space, and a certain concept of the visual public realm. Which at last brings us to architecture. People in the last ten years have been concerned with how to define space so that it encourages diversity and sociability. The basic political issue for these new urban designers, as it has been for theorists of the city like myself, is the relationship between domination and spatial design. Let me read you a passage from Colin Rowe and Fred Koetter's article "Collage City" in the *Architectural Review* of August 1975. They write of the design of Hadrian's Villa, a complex of buildings built between 118 and 134 AD, as follows:

> For, if Versailles may be a sketch for
> total design in a context of total politics,
> the Villa Adriana—

—attempts to dissimulate all reference to any single controlling idea.... Hadrian, who proposes the reverse of any "totality," seems only to need accumulation of the most various fragments [...]. The Villa Adriana is a miniature Rome. It plausibly reproduces all the collisions of set pieces and all the random empirical happenings which the city so lavishly exhibited [...]. it is almost certain that the uninhibited aesthetic preference of today is for the structural discontinuities and the multiple syncopated excitements which the Villa Adriana presents [...] the bias of this preference should be clear: it is better to think of an aggregation of small and even contradictory set pieces (almost like the products of different regimes) than to entertain fantasies about total and "faultless" solutions which the condition of politics can only abort.

Hadrian's Villa, Tivoli, Italy.

This made me think of a famous epigram by the novelist Donald Barthelme. He once tried to explain his creative procedures by saying the only forms he trusts are fragments. The fear of a total identity for space is in fact inevitably bound up with total power. It comes not so much out of a taste for bricolage as out of a particular perception of what space is. I would say Rowe and Koetter's concept of space is Greek—not postmodern at all, but highly classical in the following way. The best definition I know of this concept of space was made by the German philosopher Martin Heidegger in an article called "Building, Dwelling, Thinking." The article was written in 1954 and it was translated into English in 1971 in a collection of essays called *Poetry, Language, Thought*. Heidegger writes:

> What the word for space, *Raum*, *Rum*, designates is said by its ancient meaning. *Raum* means a place cleared or freed for settlement and lodging. A space is something that has been made room for. Something that is cleared and freely named within a boundary, Greek *peras*. A boundary is not that at which something stops but, as the Greeks recognized, the boundary is that from which something *begins its presencing*. That is why the concept is that of *horismos*, that is, of the horizon, the boundary. Space is in essence that for which room has been made.

Thus:

> Space is in essence that for which room has
> been made, that which is let into its bounds.
> That for which room is made is always granted
> and hence is joined, that is, gathered, by virtue
> of a location, that is, by such a thing as the
> bridge. *Accordingly, spaces receive their being
> from locations and not from "space."*

In other words, the notion of space as bounding something or
containing something is all wrong for Heidegger. Rather, for
him, space is a clearing away for activities to happen in. And
the result of that clearing away is inevitably fragmentation. I
believe that this Greek concept of space has reappeared in our
own era as an accusation of the dominant form of space-making.
As long ago as the 1920s, philosophers understood that this
concept of space was, for instance, totally at odds with the kinds
of simplistic space-time juncture one finds in Sigfried Gideon's
Space, Time and Architecture, in which both vectors can be
measured in numbers. I think it's important to realize this. For
Husserl, for instance, the experience of being in space is what
you've made room for in your head, which differs from simply
one's physical location, as Gideon asserted. Space in this phe-
nomenologic view inevitably morphs into place.

Rowe and Koetter give us exactly the sense of that morphing in describing Hadrian's Villa. The building makes us feel subjectively that it has been there over a much longer period than it in fact was. They say that many regimes seem to have been present in this place because many hands were involved in its making. Collage is a dominant sensibility of modern writing. So, in Rowe and Koetter's example, and in the attempt to articulate that sense of space philosophically, and in Heidegger and Husserl, collage can be created from nothing but the form. If space morphs into place, time will be disoriented and the illusion of overlay of historical depth will be created. If you fragment a built form, you can make it seem much older than it is. This is at a totally different level of complexity and subtlety than the kinds of theories of space-time continuum described by Gideon.

I stress this metamorphosis for three reasons. First, we're dealing here with modern architects' attempt to confront the meaning of time. It's not historicism in the sense of making historical quotes, as Philip Johnson does in the AT&T building, or that Charles Moore does in the Piazza d'Italia in New Orleans. This is confronting something much deeper. Second, the experience of time as fabricated in space contests the Haussmannian notions of space we explored in the first lecture. The radical reaction to total plans imposed by a political regime cannot be a total plan created or voted by a people or anyone else. Instead there's a deconstructive reaction to borrow a piece of fashionable literary jargon. Space that makes room for living by fragmenting itself, and so producing an illusion of the length of habitation. The move Koetter and Rowe argue for is important in the third way, which connects with the theme of our last lecture. In that lecture, we explored the social and political dangers of the community that identifies itself. Here we see designers worrying about spatial identity for the same reason and suggesting that good urban space will create something beyond an easily recognizable identity and a clear image. What the principle expressed in "Collage City" has to do with the social psychology of urban life. The problem is how a sense of space beyond identity can be created. How do you create today the equivalent of Hadrian's Villa?

Piazza d'Italia (Architect: Charles Moore), New Orleans.

AT&T Building (Architects: Philip Johnson and John Burgee), 1984.

THE INCIDENTS

I think we can learn something from looking at some recent work by Aldo Rossi. He seeks to overlay a set of archetypical urban and individual building forms that have disappeared. In other words, he wants us to recall what he believes are buried archetypes of urban form that have been covered over by the processes of familiar friends and enemies—industrial capitalism. The act of recall, for Rossi, should be disorienting. Collaging these archetypical forms in the present should disorient our sense of a place. For instance, in *Oppositions* 5, 1976, Aldo Rossi sets out his practice thus. He wishes to restore the archetypical, essential forms of the historical city and thereby restore collective memory. This becomes possible, Rossi contends, if we see "memory...[as] the connecting thread of the...structure of [the city]...[so that] urban facts arrange themselves into the same urban structure. Within this structure, memory becomes the conscience of the city." That is, the capacity of an architect to arouse his archetypical memory of forms that have disappeared, that we don't see, becomes an act of disorienting. ———— Rossi had in mind an essay by Adolf Loos written in 1910 called *Architecture*, which declared that "has recognized that most modern programs are inappropriate vehicles for architecture, and for him this has meant having recourse to a so-called analogical architecture, whose reference and elements are to be abstracted from the vernacular in the broadest possible sense."

All admirable in theory, but not in practice. A particular structure that Rossi built attempts to create a disorienting collage of memory—a provocation in space—and seems to have absolutely failed to create the sense of *Raum*, of a living place. It's the large school at Fagnano Olona built between 1972 and 1976. The school is basically shaped like a set of toy boxes, with an animal-like spine: one part morphing into a circular, almost silo-like structure at the ground level. You approach the school over perhaps the hottest and dustiest road in Italy and come to a greenhouse without windows, a long, low structure. You walk through the greenhouse, and you approach a kind of structure that's pure white; its windows have absolutely no ornament. They're set in like prison block windows. The children walk through this structure—and they're cautioned not to wander around inside this greenhouse without glass—to a designated play area in front of this round, silo-like area, which is supposed to recall in their minds a kind of twelfth-century campanile. I've spent a good deal of time at this school: it is certainly disorienting.

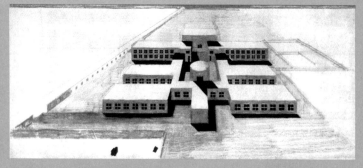

**Perspective for Scuola elementare a Fagnano Olona, Italy
(Architect: Aldo Rossi), 1972–76.**

View of Scuola elementare a Fagnano Olona with children, Italy, c. 1976.

Scuola elementare a Fagnano Olona, photo taken 2011.

THE INCIDENTS

The results on the children are remarkable. It's interesting to look at the publicity photos that Rossi gave to Dan Graham for this article in *ArtForum*. The kids are running around playing ball, and they look absolutely incongruous at play in the space because the space is in fact the archetypal space of a cemetery. The kids are indeed disoriented; they're constantly looking for places to hide, so that, for instance, all the play goes on at the outer exterior corners of the building, where they can't be seen, at the most marginal part of the schoolyard-cemetery. The designated play area in the center is abandoned. So, too, the children have to be rigidly disciplined to walk through the greenhouse without glass—they walk around it, and they persistently try to deface its walls. Why should this be? Rossi has succeeded in creating a kind of disoriented space, which means that one feels one is transported back in the realm of the dead. Much more so than at a nearby Roman ruin at Fagnano Olona. For me, this notion that what one recovers by that sense of history—it's why he designed so many cemeteries—is what makes this architecture so clear as a collage—arbitrarily. The kids live in it, but hate it.

This is a problem in Rossi's sculpture—I mean, it's very moving and it's a tragic building to visit, but not to inhabit. On a more superficial level you could say the same thing of Venturi, or someone like Charles Moore; they're trivial examples of the same sort of dead quoting. In our seminars we've called this *symbolic reference*: the reference is made by someone who doesn't live in its forms. Rossi's impulse is to bring the space alive, when, in fact, what happens is that it becomes literally embalmed. To be fair to Rossi, his drawings are not at all like this—for instance, the drawings that were exhibited in New York a couple of years ago are filled with life. Something goes wrong between the drawing and the building itself. ———— I pay so much attention to this wrong road because it exemplifies exactly the defeat we have to avoid, which is orienting imagery, or, put more abstractly, a place whose forms are derived from the identity of an image.

Aldo Rossi, Cimiterio di San Cataldo, Modena.

The town square, which I sketched for you, values process over fixed, clear form. The same thing is true visually. How do you then visually design a process? Leon Krier and Robert Krier are two architects who have recently been most concerned with defining process. There's a little statement of Leon's about their work that I believe embodies exactly the problematic that people who want to make this community visually are involved in. He says of their work, and particularly their work in Luxembourg:

> That we try in our projects to reestablish the
> dialectic of building and public realm, of solid
> and void, the built organism and the space it
> necessarily creates around itself.

Which leads to the declaration that I want to emphasize:

> The architectural language we use
> for fairly large urban parts is both simple
> and ambiguous.

The question is how that ambiguity can be designed. His brother, Robert, tried to do so as what he called *linking forms*. As an example, in a Rome project that puts simple roofs over the ends of open-air squares, they put up absolutely huge columns that are filled with things like offices and shops, and they hold up a roof that covers the whole square, and all the activity that was formerly in the square is sucked up into the building. Rob Krier is very interesting about this. He says:

> I want the huge pillars to carry the roof, to house rooms for a new social center open 24 hours a day, which allows restaurants, clubs, rooms for games and artistic performances.

He hopes these social centers will—

> —replace institutions like the Church and municipo and finally the school.

In other words, what's involved is that you attempt to create a kind of place for a gradual, tremendously utopian, new public social form through an architectural disorientation of a classical spatial form. It's poles apart from Rossi. Critics say they're both postmodernists, but the concept of form is much more proactive than Rossi's. What Leon wants to do is absolutely vitiate the innate meaning of any of those historic urban references. The square space as a geometry loses meaning in their project—instead the tremendous columns make it possible to imagine life proceeds, unplanned, underneath.

Leon Krier, Roma Interotta, social center in St. Peter's Square; in background, Piazza Navona and Via Corso, Rome, 1977.

Leon Krier, drawing for The New Rome Centers, project for St. Peter's Square, Rome, 1979.

DEMOCRACY AND URBAN FORM   217

Walden 7 (Architect: Ricardo Bofill), Barcelona, 1975.

THE INCIDENTS

Whether the Kriers' idea is good or not, I want to point out something about the procedure that I believe is typical of a lot of work being done now in the attempt to create and plan public spaces. This work, like much of what it typifies, assumes that renovation of the social public occurs through an act of visual disorientation. That is, you bring this stuff together, and if the renovation works, then the activities in the building ought to spill out beyond it. This goes back to what we were talking about earlier in this lecture. The building form will not be so much eclipsed, then, as much as it will become distinct from the forms of living it arouses. The Kriers are absolutely willing to admit this, but there are many architects who aren't and who've assumed that the task of articulating public space is to create a container that holds everything. Renovation of the public realm requires, as Rob says, architecture that "bleeds." I refer you in this regard to Ricardo Bofill's Walden Seven building in Barcelona, completed in 1976. What Ricardo did was brilliant. He put up a series of towers, and at the base he put in all the services for structures to be built in a kind of camp around these towers. He said he wanted the buildings to extend themselves geographically like mushrooms growing around the base of the building. The architectural provision—for the street level and even up to the second level—is to be erased as an image by whatever these very concentrated and dense "mushrooms" grow.

This review suggests six principles by which a complex town square can be physically designed. The first is the most obvious: there has to be a reevaluation of the relationship between space and motion. When we talked about Baron Haussmann's work in Paris, we said that the fundamental aspect of that plan was its attempt to make space contingent upon motion in a total and comprehensive way. Ideas of space as presented by people like Heidegger and the like are about anti-Haussmannization—that is, space that is built for use apart from the traffic that it permits to go through it. To put this in very concrete terms, the flow of traffic is something that is much less important than the space making room for changing ways of living. ——— The second principle is that there be no fixed-function streets. The only way you can have freedom is by removing the notion of fixed function from the street, which is true also of how buildings meet. For example, the lobbies of a lot of international-style buildings being put up in Chicago have no functions at all. The lobby is an entrance into life, which is at least forty feet off the ground. There's just glass and beautiful travertine. It's a way of fixing the function on the street so that nothing can happen. I believe this problem is absolutely fatal to attempts create a more livable public space. You can only have that space if the space is subject to a change in function.

Exterior view of the IBM Building (Architect: Mies van der Rohe), Chicago, 1972.

The third of these six principles is that there would be revisable imagery in the building as a whole as functions shift. This is one way of partially dealing with Rossi's problem—that is, if one sees that the children want to tear the structure down, the form should let them try changing it. The building can be revised by its use. That's very difficult for architects to accept. Very difficult. You want to deny us—if I may make this adversarial—the freedom of revision. But you can't have a public realm unless a building's imagery can be revised by its citizens. The moment you assert a notion of image purity, you've decided that the whole process of social exchange in that building is meaningless. I'll give you a very sad example of this. When I was a very young man Eero Saarinen took me to a house he had built, and in the kitchen there were some very sharp corners on the kitchen counters. I said, "Mr. Saarinen, what if a child running around a corner," I mean they're sort of prow-like corners, "hits his head?" And he said, "Well, one of two things could happen. Either they'll learn not to hit their heads or they'll abandon the house." That is exactly what destroys the notion of any kind of citizen agency.

Derived from this is that the technology of building form has to be articulated in such a way that it can be comprehended by somebody who is not a designer, and therefore entered into the realm of discourse. I think, for instance, Moshe, of your Habitat structures, which are capable of being discussed because the technology is evident. You can't have flexible public space if you have mystifying building technology. Technological transparency enables citizen participation. If I, or somebody else who is not an architect can't understand how a form is made, then the space becomes abstract. If one is serious about building public space, I think there has to be a revolution in the kinds of technical engineering and approaches to creating—even if it's just the way a facade is mounted, or the way in which electricity is deployed on the street—that are understandable and therefore discussable by the people who use that space. ——— And, derived from the fourth, the fifth principle is that building forms can extend themselves. The mushroom is Bofill's solution to Krier's difficulty, it's a specific way to design a process. We need to experiment with other ways buildings can provide for their own extension.

The last principle is the one I'm most confused about, which is how to spatially articulate division between public and private realms. There are three components to this problem: separation of family and work, separation of family and commerce, and what we called in the first lecture the *campusization* of instrumental activities. Currently, thick, deep lines separate these realms; we need more ambitious lines. There does need to be a separation but not a rigid barrier, particularly not to make the family an isolated realm. The question is how to make a more ambitious, porous separation. This is something I'm about to spend two or three years on. ———— In conclusion, I want to try to tie all of this material together. To design a town square we have to refer to issues of stimulation and desensitization that we explored in the third lecture. Remember that we talked about the assumption by people like Georg Simmel and Walter Benjamin that the greater the density, crowding, and public life of the city, the more stimulation there was. The domain of the public is the domain of the stimulated, the domain of the private is the domain of the destimulization. Today we've been looking at ways diversity can in fact fragment stimuli as much as provoke it.

We've been trying to look at more abstract and systematic ways that the conditions under which the existence of diversity create a kind of diffusion of certain kinds of stimuli. In a practical application, my team is studying what happens to people who have been formerly violent in mental hospitals when they're put into community halfway houses. It's the difference between recovery in a suburb or recovery in Greenwich Village. What we're finding is that the very diversity of a New York life—the very kind of complexity of stimuli—seems to act on these people so that they're much less likely to be taken over by their own personal problems. It's a very complicated subject, and I barely understand all of it, but I mention it because the city turns people more outward than does a simple environment. That is, public life might form the relief from troubles in private life.

Another way of understanding outwardly focused experience in a city concerns religion. One of my students for instance is thinking about the negative utopia of public squares without churches. It seemed wrong to him that when he started his study that religious enthusiasm should be fragmented, but found that participation in church life was quite intense in urban churches; the stimulus of the square carried over into the chancel. The point I'm trying to bring up here is that it seems the sixth area, or principle, that a planning strategy for articulating public and private space has to look at is stimulation as spilling over social as well as visual boundaries. ———— I've listed the six principles of what I believe are design requisites for building this kind of community of difference: the reevaluation of the relationship between space and motion; the importance of no fixed-function street fronts; revisable imagery in buildings as functions shift or as discourse decides to change them; a technology of building form that can be articulated in such a way that it can be comprehended by someone who is not a designer and therefore become discursive; the building form that can extend itself; and, finally, the articulation of public–private differences that don't consider the private as a refuge from the public but rather the other way around.

The city that emerges from what we've discussed in this lecture may seem a strange place—strange because we've lost our way urbanistically. We've arrived at a critical moment of rupture in the design of cities and in their habitation. Economic and political forces of nineteenth-century society destroyed livable cities in our own century. We're the heirs of that great drama of nineteenth-century urbanism, and we weren't left the culture of Balzac, the drama itself, or the complexity of social fabric in great tension, but merely the techniques for destroying this tension—the techniques for massive segregation, isolation, and identity-making. So we've been deprived of cities. This deprivation has not accidentally sent designers in the last decade in search of the usable past. In some cases, like Charles Moore, the search is for the bric-a-brac of past forms. For more serious and more socially minded designers, it's for a principle of history, either a principle of time and collage, as for Koetter and Rowe, or of archetypical memory, as for Rossi. On the one side, then, we've attempted to recover cities by recovering a historical imagination of them, to create a sense of difference and disruption in the cities we know.

The other side of this coin—as I hope I've made clear in my critique of Rossi and presentation of my abstract requisite rules and concrete requirements for a community of difference—is that the experience of time is not the experience of something past, something embalmed. A radical rupture—in particular with older notions of being linked to other people—has come to separate us irremediably from people who've lived in organically bound *Gemeinschaft* communities, or communities of ascribed identity. The town square requires us to break the mindset of the image archetypes we still have. What I've been trying to say through these five lectures—and this is the most schematic and therefore perhaps least compelling form—is that something really new has to be made out of all the fragments of city life. In this moment of such bankruptcy of thinking about what it means to inhabit a dense, diverse, intermixed place, we have to begin to explore what it means for a human being to prize a sense of selfhood and to be without simple identity-based community—I see that as a great opportunity to live beyond that boundary—and yet to be in contact with other people. That's how life in the town square should be. Urban design can help make it happen. ——— Thank you very much.

DEMOCRATIC THEORY AND URBAN FORM

MOSHE: Since this is the last of the six lectures of "Democracy and Urban Form" I thought it would be appropriate, not to make an introduction and not a summary either, but perhaps to say a couple of things about the impact these lectures and Richard's visits to the school have had. I think it's quite common for social scientists to delve into the past and try to relate the forms of cities to the social and economic and political phenomena that created them. It is less common for social scientists to attempt to look at the present and try to relate the existing city that we live in to some of the social forces that created them; it is even less common for social scientists to look forward and try and tell us what certain physical design decisions might bring about as consequence. Richard Sennett has attempted to do all three. It is for that reason we appreciate this series. This is all happening in the context of a renewed interest in studying city form in the past but with equal interest in trying to understand what brought those forms about. The lectures, seminars, and reviews we've had over the semester added a dimension to the way in which students in the School have been looking at cities.

RICHARD: I will be brief tonight, I promise, so we can all go have a drink. I'd just like to thank you, Moshe, for inviting me to these lectures. They're preliminary thoughts, and I've particularly appreciated the people who've come to the discussions in the mornings after them. ———— I want to assay tonight what cities have to do with politics and political theory. I'd first point out that we make a connection between freedom of speech and being a free person. This is a very recent connection in Western history. The Greeks divorced the two: words were but a means to action; war and peace mattered more. The right to speak freely as constituting freedom is something that goes back about 230 to 235 years, as a doctrine. It's the most recent definition of freedom that we have, and it's the most fragile.

To guarantee people the right of free expression by writing it down on a piece of paper is not a very secure freedom, and especially for this freedom. The culture of modern cities, as I've tried to show, can strengthen the right to discourse with others. In the modern city, moreover, architecture can help strengthen personal expression in the practices of everyday life. The right to free expression can literally be built in the form of the city. In the very fabric of the city, and in the construction, particularly, of spaces for verbal exchange with people unlike oneself.

In these lectures we've asked how a city could embody freedom of expression. How could it be planned? And conversely, what are the pressures against realizing this ideal in the modern city? In the first three lectures, we looked at three forces that might inhibit free discourse in the way modern cities are organized. In the first lecture, we looked at the way in which forces of domination, in particular forces of rational domination, might inhibit free discourse by associating the notion of order with the notion of isolation; poor old Baron Haussmann, I'm afraid, has become a whipping boy for this evil. More largely, many of our notions about order as embodied in the modern city are notions of separating potentially hostile groups from contact with each other. Their silence creates order. That attempt to create silence in the city is obviously the first and most fundamental way this culture of free expression might be inhibited.

In the second lecture, we looked at why people might be willing to be silenced, and how that desire might lead them to impose a mute tyranny on themselves. That's why we went through this long analysis of Alexis de Tocqueville. It would be much too simplistic to say that people are burning to have free and open expression with people unlike themselves, and the only reason they don't have it is that the forces—all those naughty enemies—capitalist, rationalist domination—are keeping them from speaking. Instead, we looked at a situation in which people's unhappiness leads them to seek isolation from other people. It's a peculiar situation. Equality in cultural values makes people unhappy. We looked at why the very unhappiness of modern egalitarian society might push people, perversely, to search for separation from one another.

And in the third lecture, we looked at what I think is probably the most difficult proposition to make sense of. This is a distinctly urban version of freedom based on the toleration of difference. We compared the notion of corporate freedom that existed in the medieval German city, in the city of the Hanseatic League of the thirteenth century, with a more personal freedom in the modern city. This emerged from the discussion of Georg Simmel and Walter Benjamin. On the one hand, both agree the dense and diverse city does promote awareness of others who are unlike oneself, but this conscious awareness devalues verbal interchange. So the third of these forces working against free expression can be described as visual and bodily consciousness of the other that supplants discourse as a constitutive element of urban culture. Toleration of difference works at cross purposes with discourse about differences. ——— So, these three forces work quite strongly against incarnating in the very form of the city this right, this fragile right, to openly express yourself to those who are different from you.

Then, in the fourth lecture, we looked at the idea of a town square—the public space where discourse should happen. That is, one might think of a possible form of open discussion that would transcend communication with people who are like oneself—which I called a *community of identity*. We drew a contrast between the old ethnic community and a new civic formation. We referred to the ideas of Orlando Patterson about those old, ascriptive communities of identity. How to cast off the burden of ascription, or of feeling free to talk only with other people who are like oneself? That's the problem the modern town square faces.

This led us, in the previous lecture, to consider how to build a place in which people who differ are talking to each other. We saw that this required a complicated set of rules, both abstract and concrete, that would have to govern any kind of city and community planning. The essence of building a community of difference appeared by rethinking two elements of the city. One was the sense of space—and we discussed that in terms of the concept of space as it appeared in Martin Heidegger and in so-called postmodernist architects like Fred Koetter and Colin Rowe. The second element was how the divide between public and private space would have to be reconstituted in order to create forums for discourse. This led us, at the end of the last lecture, to lay out six rules of community planning to build physically and visually a kind of environment in which talk might proceed. ———— Today I want to pose two problems about the intellectual journey we've taken. The first of them is pretty obvious: how does it happen that the city of our first four lectures, in which expression between people who are unlike is so difficult, is also the same material city of this last lecture, in which we glimpsed a possibility for expression between people who are unlike? Both cities are made of brick, concrete, glass, and steel. Secondly, what is the substance of urban, democratic discourse? What are people talking about?

I'll try to answer both questions by making a very concrete contrast. A contrast between being a lawyer in Paris in 1781 versus being a lawyer in New York in 1981, not in terms of practicing the law but in terms of one's everyday experience of talking. How would the form of the city affect the lawyers' experience of free expression? I choose Paris in 1781 for a fairly obvious reason—because it's in the 1760s that for the first time people began asserting the right to freedom of expression in ordinary social life and not merely in the organized polity— for instance, in 1759 they began demanding that police reports no longer be given on what was said in the salons. Before that, people expected police spies in their homes if they had a large gathering. Suddenly, you have a beginning of a change to that in 1759. And by 1781, that is, by 200 years ago, a lawyer, or a rather garrulous, opinionated doctor—I thought of this character as having all sorts of attributes—would feel rather comfortable saying what he thought to other people outside an organized legal setting. I'd like to contrast what that comfort is like to the notion of freedom of expression that a lawyer, again outside the office, might experience in 1981 in New York.

The first contrast we would make is that our Paris lawyer in 1781 would understand freedom of expression as a declaration— an act of will by the speaker. He would understand himself to be free to express what he felt as an assertive act. To assert himself, our salon lawyer would coin phrases in advice and perhaps practice them before a mirror. It's a very different situation from my model New York lawyer, in which freedom of expression, again outside his job, is something that can just come, speech that is more informal, more spontaneous. I remind you of W. H. Auden's famous statement about New York, that the city is "an open door, through which one didn't realize one had walked." Much of what we mean by freedom of expression has to do with that sense of spur of the moment. That is, the more spontaneous the expression can be, the freer it is, and the more expressive the will can be consciously and artfully shaped. There's that shift in speech that defines the difference between the two eras of expression—the emphasis on will that shifts to an emphasis on spontaneity.

The city set the context for this shift. In Paris in 1781, the people in a salon, or lower down in a cafe like the Café Procope, knew one another. For instance, the salon of Madame Necker. Hers was a very prominent bourgeois family we happen to know a lot about, because Monsieur Necker was a finance guru widely consulted by Parisians. Everybody tried to write down what Monsieur Necker was saying because they were convinced he had this economic wisdom. He was one of those people who often said of other people's misfortune, "If only they'd listened to me." His wife and daughter—his daughter was Madame De Stael—ran a famous salon. There our lawyer would have had great pleasure mixing with others, his expressions presenting a fixed face—one's public face. If I can put this formally, the conditions of social exchange in Paris toward the end of the eighteenth century were not linked to a notion of personal vulnerability. Once you've decided to speak, you talk to other people who also have decided to speak, you donned a mask.

Whereas the community of expression we know now admits personal vulnerability. What you say to somebody else by opening up freely might express an inner wound, or a personal feeling that others might turn against. Our lawyer is not in court. Outside it, at a party, he may let his hair down. And we want him to do so, we want to know who he really is. ——— My old teacher, David Riesman, once put this very nicely. He said that in modern society, an inner-directed formal person is somebody indifferent to other people. Conversely, becoming open and sensitive to other people means that you leave yourself open to being potentially vulnerable to them. This is the risk of being free. These ways of discoursing are the cultural contrast that I would make between my lawyer in 1781 and my lawyer in 1981.

The third contrast is related spaces of encounter. These were tightly controlled in the eighteenth-century salons, which relied on gatekeeping a strict admission. The space of the salon was tightly bounded rather than porous. Whereas the spaces of exchange in New York are fluid and open due to incursions, mobility, and chance presence. That is, there is an emphasis, again, on spontaneity. We've put a premium on the notion on chance encounter as changing discourse with the Other; the space required for things to happen requires loose boundaries. What's happened in the modern city is a growing contradiction between the economic and administrative structures of the city and the structures of communication. The economic and administrative structure of the modern city is all about coherent control. Our lawyer wants to free himself from this discipline— out of court. He would be an embarrassing figure in the salon.

Put less novelistically, and more abstractly, there is a contradiction between the economy and the culture of modern cities. Here lies one of the most famous theorems in the whole history of our discipline of urban studies. It's by Louis Wirth. Louis Wirth was a sociologist who studied in Germany, who studied with Simmel before the First World War and then studied with Robert E. Park, and he and Park started the famous Chicago School of Urban Studies in the 1920s and 1930s at the University of Chicago. Wirth argued that in modern society, division of labor is everywhere, but in cities has accelerated. It's accelerated because—and this goes back to our discussion about scale—of the multiplier effect. If you have an IBM that's out in Scarsdale and another IBM or General Electric that's in Trenton, the actions and dealings these two firms have with each other produce X amount of specialized roles. If they're right next to each other or across the street, the fact that they're so close together produces synergies but also a greater division of labor. Duplicated jobs are eliminated but more specialized jobs are created. Socially the consequence is the roles of people in the city become more segmented. Not just that their jobs are divided up, but that their whole experience in the city becomes more partial and particularized. A "Black father" means different things when the father walks in the neighborhood, goes to a concert, shops downtown, attends a union meeting; his self becomes differently shaded in each of these settings. A large city multiplies the settings.

I'd like to take Wirth's idea a step further—indeed, my theory of the city is based on taking it a step further—to say that this multiplication becomes contradictory in form. In my view this growing complexity is good. That is to say, the result of this multiplier effect creates new channels of social communication that transcend the mere process of managing more efficiently. As in business, there are communication synergies. Unlike business—or perhaps not—the more variety of roles and discourses, the more discordant they become. The city opens, if I can put this formally, social channels more complicated than those necessary to perform a function.

That's what's wrong in urban terms with Weber's famous notion of the iron cage of bureaucracy. Weber's notion of the iron cage depicted people in a prison of rules, but all they can do is shake the bars. In a city, the bars can crack, as it were. In Wirth's terms, cities develop human beings who become bigger than any one of their social roles. I'm no Pollyanna about this, I'm merely saying cities can help people see beyond their own cages. Urban freedom begins just when they do. That's why I've never believed in any kind of economic functionalism when you deal with cities. It's the essential quality and the tragedy of urban life precisely that people can develop in a milieu where they are subject to domination in any one rule yet see beyond it.

———— It's for this reason I argue that the possibility of creating an urban politics based on the culture of urban life, based especially on the fragmenting of self in the city. That's all I would claim for this politics. Put a little more simply, a possibility cities give people is a taste for the kind of freedom that might ultimately be marshalled against the very structures of domination they have to live under.

The second thing I want to articulate in this short lecture is the relationship of that kind of urban culture to the substance of discourse itself. What happens to the actual discourse when city culture is not one of common ground but of fragmentation and segmentation? This question reflects a major shift in social philosophy now. Truth is a very different matter when it's set in the context of discourse than when it's set outside it. Think about a Platonic dialog, for instance the statement that Glaucon makes at the end of the ninth book of *The Republic*: he says something like "all of this state has existed solely because we have been able to talk with each other." That is, nobody could think it out for themselves. It's only because we've been able to talk to each other that that's happened. A major school of social philosophy in the twentieth century is trying to reclaim this sense of discursive truth. I suppose the two leading figures in it are Hans Georg Gadamer and, in a slightly different way, Jürgen Habermas.

The twists and turns of discussion are central to understanding the truth of what people say. In the work of Habermas, the effect of domination is to distort discourse. This seems like a self-evident point, but I'll give an example of what he's worried about. Possessive individualism makes us defend our beliefs as though they were possessions. That's why we feel vulnerable when somebody challenges us—think of our New York lawyer. He will resist, we will resist, if thoughts are like things we own. We don't give our cars or houses away freely. Beliefs are possessions, they define our selves. And therefore, if we change our beliefs, we are changing or losing some part of our self. If we have to change our ideas because some part of them is diminished, that's the kind of thing that Habermas is worried about. But the urban condition loosens this possessiveness we are gaining as well as losing in our discourse.

The content of discourse, Gadamer asserts, is demeaned by reification. Simply put, reification is the conversion of a specific person or truth between two people into a condition that is universal and having the status of a natural fact. If, for instance, Moshe and I have a discussion about Arabs in Jerusalem in 1981, and then I take away from that discussion that that's the way Islam is, and then I convert that's the way Islam is to that's the way human beings are, I have succeeded in reifying the conditions of discourse. It's by imprisoning people in the reified world that you are able to control them. Racism works by reification; each Black human being is treated as an example of a type; the legal system deals in types, in generalized cases; it reifies in order to make general rules. The last part of Gadamer's *Truth and Method* shows how reification is the great modern tool of dominating the minds of those who are controlled as well as their actions. Gadamer and Habermas relate to Plato. For Plato, reification occurs because men have failed to submit the conditions of their lives to discourse. As Socrates says in *Phaedrus* for instance, discourse is like a sort of a healing treatment. You can't reify as long as you're discursive. For Gadamer and Habermas, however, reification occurs in discourse. The disease enters into talk. And the problem is how to change it and break it down by creating new conditions of discourse.

Here is where I think the modern city enters as a possible agent for change. People who live in a segmented world of discourse— people who change their persona as they move through their days, whose speech situation changes as their roles change, who have all that segmentation—all of this offers a kind of weapon against reification. It's very hard to treat other people as reified natural categories if you're constantly changing your relationship with them. So that the more segmentation proceeds as a process, the more differentiation proceeds, there results, I would argue, in a greater possibility for freedom of discourse in which reification can be broken down. Or to speak jargon—I'm sorry, I hate speaking social science jargon, but this is worth using— you have a demystification of universalization. In other words, you demystify the notion of a representative person that you're speaking to. You no longer believe in that reified fact. Therein lies a possibility for a new kind of democracy in cities. For that reason I believe that the stimulation of difference in cities by the tools that we talked about in the previous lecture ultimately serves the cause of liberation. The more breakdown of that segmented way there is, and the more exposure to the other there is, the more we begin undoing the work that I believe the modern state has become so proficient in ideologically, which is reification. By encouraging experiences of Otherness, fragmentation, contradiction, and dissonance in city life, we can contest the larger culture of domination.

I want to end these six lectures on what I think will seem to you a rather odd note. It's something that I've been thinking a lot: Who is this demystified being? Or, to put it another way, isn't a man without illusions a man without qualities? I don't mean to be autobiographical, but I published a book called *The Uses of Disorder*, and I had a long discussion with Jean Paul Sartre after it came out. He said something to me that absolutely floored me. He said, "I want to believe you, but I believe that human character is only formed out of illusion. And that what you are recommending is a kind of neutral world which would be a totally free world and a world without any human substance." This statement bowled me over, because the truth of it seemed so obvious. It's something that has sort of obsessed me for the last eleven years. I know why he said it. He was writing on Gustave Flaubert. And of course that's what happens in a sentimental education, isn't it? That education is an education that finally truth is a kind of dagger, a kind of stripping away of sentiment because it's an illusion.

The more I've thought about this, the more I think that this question Sartre asked me was wrong—not wrong, but I mean that one could give a better answer to it. It's that I think we're going to have to learn in cities to have whole new experiences of solitude in order to have a domain of sociability. I just want to introduce this idea, in place of a conclusion to these talks. There's a great difference between solitude and isolation. Isolation comes from a lack of contact with the other people. But very deep experiences of solitude come precisely out of being exposed to people who are unlike yourself and feeling the distance. Feeling that you're unlike. It's very clear to me, both in studying life histories and thinking abstractly, that people who have very diverse experiences in cities have a kind of solitude, and know a kind of solitude in themselves by knowing that they're just one among many, and that there are many there. Hannah Arendt once expressed this at the end of *The Origins of Totalitarianism* by quoting a distinction that I think Epictetus made between solitude and isolation. Epictetus said, "Isolation occurs when a person feels deprived of other people, and solitude occurs when a person feels that they are exposed to people who they can't understand." In modern cities we are going to have to come to terms with the new order of solitude. ———— Thank you very much.

Contributors

RICHARD SENNETT grew up in the Cabrini Green housing project in Chicago, attended the Julliard School in New York, and then studied social relations at Harvard. Over the last five decades, he has written about social life in cities, changes in labor and social theory. His books include *The Hidden Injuries of Class*, *The Fall of Public Man*, *The Corrosion of Character*, *The Culture of the New Capitalism*, *The Craftsman* and *Building and Dwelling*. Sennett has advised the United Nations on urban issues for the past thirty years and currently serves as member of the UN Committee on Urban Initiatives. Among other awards, he has received the Hegel Prize, the Spinoza Prize, and the Centennial Medal from Harvard University.

DIANE E. DAVIS is the Charles Dyer Norton Professor of Regional Development and Urbanism and former Chair of the Department of Urban Planning and Design at the Harvard GSD. Before moving to the GSD in 2011, Davis served as the head of the International Development Group in the Department of Urban Studies and Planning at MIT, where she also was Associate Dean of the School of Architecture and Planning. After a year teaching in social studies at Harvard, she started her academic career at the Graduate Faculty of the New School for Social Research where she held a joint appointment in sociology and historical studies. Trained as a sociologist with an interest in political geography (BA Northwestern University, PhD UCLA), Davis's research interests include the relations between urbanization and national development, urban governance, informality, and the growth and structure of cities in the Global South, with a special emphasis on Latin America and on questions of political power, sovereignty, urban violence, and police impunity. Current projects include an examination of conflict cities, spatial strategies for political mobilization, and territories at risk.

MOSHE SAFDIE is an architect, urban planner, educator, theorist, and author. Embracing a comprehensive and humane design philosophy, Safdie is committed to architecture that supports and enhances a project's program; that is informed by the geographic, social, and cultural elements that define a place; and that responds to human needs and aspirations.

Over a celebrated sixty-year career, Safdie has explored the essential principles of socially responsible design with a distinct visual language. With completed projects in North and South America, the Middle East, and Asia, his wide range of built work includes cultural, educational, and civic institutions; neighborhoods and public parks; housing; mixed-use urban centers; airports; as well as master plans for existing communities and entirely new cities.

A citizen of Israel, Canada, and the United States, Safdie has been recognized globally with honors that include the Companion of the Order of Canada; the Gold Medal from both the Royal Architectural Institute of Canada and the American Institute of Architects; the National Design Award for Lifetime Achievement by the Cooper Hewitt Smithsonian; and the Wolf Prize in Architecture.

Colophon

Richard Sennett
Democracy and Urban Form

Series editors: Ken Stewart and Marielle Suba
Image assistance: Ava Danieu
Design: ELLA with Gabrielle Pulgar
Printing: Grafiche Veneziane, Italy

ISBN 978-1-915609-47-2

Distributed by The MIT Press, Art Data, Les presses du réel, and Idea Books

Every effort has been made to contact the rightful owners with regard to copyrights and permissions. We apologize for any inadvertent errors or omissions.

Published by
Harvard Design Press   Sternberg Press
48 Quincy Street   71–75 Shelton Street
Cambridge, MA 02138   UK–London WC2H 9JQ
gsd.harvard.edu   www.sternberg-press.com

Harvard Design Press is the book imprint of the Harvard University Graduate School of Design.

The Incidents

The Architecture of Taste
Pierre Hermé

Freedom of Use
Anne Lacaton and Jean-Philippe Vassal

Abstract from the Concrete
David Harvey

Architectural Ethnography
Atelier Bow-Wow

Design Thinking in the Digital Age
Peter G. Rowe

"Insert Complicated Title Here"
Virgil Abloh

Beyond the Collaboration
Sterling Ruby and Raf Simons

Design in a Frame of Emotion
Hannah Beachler with Jacqueline Stewart and Toni L. Griffin

Inhabiting the Negative Space
Jenny Odell

A Rage in Harlem: June Jordan and Architecture
Nikil Saval

Posthuman Knowledge and the Critical Posthumanities
Rosi Braidotti